T0129071

A Portrait of *Mommy*

Expressions of Love, Faith, and Perseverance

J. L. COSTON

ARCHWAY
PUBLISHING

Archway Publishing books may be ordered through booksellers or by contacting:

Archway Publishing
1663 Liberty Drive
Bloomington, IN 47403
www.archwaypublishing.com
1 (888) 242-5904

Because of the dynamic nature of the Internet, any web addresses or links contained in this book may have changed since publication and may no longer be valid. The views expressed in this work are solely those of the author and do not necessarily reflect the views of the publisher, and the publisher hereby disclaims any responsibility for them.

Any people depicted in stock imagery provided by Thinkstock are models, and such images are being used for illustrative purposes only. Certain stock imagery © Thinkstock.

ISBN: 978-1-4808-5733-9 (sc)
ISBN: 978-1-4808-5732-2 (hc)
ISBN: 978-1-4808-5180-1 (e)

Library of Congress Control Number: 2017915753

Print information available on the last page.

Archway Publishing rev. date: 01/18/2018

CONTENTS

ACKNOWLEDGMENTS

I wrote this book to honor my dear, precious mother, Ellawese Darden, affectionately known as *Mommy*. She is a picture of beauty on the inside and out, shining as a light in this dark world. When I see her humanity and compassion for others, I truly believe it's impossible for me to measure up to her. My mother is a gift from God Almighty, who has put His imprint on the earth through her hands. What a tremendous example for me, our family, friends, and community. I love you, Mommy, and pray this book will bless you and inspire you to continue to live a victorious life through Jesus Christ! At eighty-eight years old, your light is needed now more than ever!

PREFACE

WRITING ABOUT MOMMY IS IMPORTANT TO ME because she has a wealth of knowledge and information about our family's history. She has talked with me and others over the years about the adventures of her life, and I never want her stories forgotten. Although I had no intention to ever write another book after *"Escape to Pray!"* I surprised myself after being told by a prophet some years later that I would be writing one more. To my amazement, I had the idea to write about my loving "Mommy." So for many days I sat with her on a weekly schedule, talked, and asked questions, recording Mommy for countless hours on an old-fashioned tape recorder, and now I'm finalizing the process.

The most valuable woman in the world to me is my Mommy. So why not document something about her? She is a woman who has given her time, money, labor and selfless acts of kindness to many people yet countless times has not received a single thank-you. I've heard people say, "we don't do good to receive praise or thank you; we do good because we know it is the right thing to do for the glory of God." That may be somewhat true but we have to remember as human beings, we are made in the image of God, and He loves praise. Therefore I believe its okay to thank people or praise their good works when appropriate.

Mommy is valuable to our entire family, and she deserves to be celebrated every day. At eighty-eight years young, it continues to be a blessing when I know I can call her for counsel or guidance. It's a blessing to eyewitness her slowing down yet still putting forth her best efforts to pick up the pastor for church, or driving members to the store, or even visiting the hospital to pray for the sick. She continues to be a blessing as she goes out to clean homes for wealthy families whom she has been serving for years or cooking for Catholic nuns at the convent, who love her dearly. This is Mommy's blessed life today!

"*A Portrait of Mommy*" tells my mother's story, which in turn gives insight to the ability to overcome trials and tribulations with the help of God Almighty. At some point each of us will have the opportunity to face personal struggles and when these trials, struggles or heartache come from "friendly fire" (family, friends, or close loved ones), they can cut deep. However, like Mommy, we can still stand with forgiveness in our hearts and have the ability to love no matter what.

Although Mommy is a mother who is considered a senior, elderly, or even old, she is sharper than any forty-four-year-old that I know and has wisdom beyond her age. She can say with the help of the Holy Spirit what has happened, what is happening now, and what will happen in the future. I just can't stop thanking God for her!

CHAPTER 1

Mommy's Story

I WAS BORN IN A SMALL COUNTRY TOWN CALLED Jacksonville, located in Telfair County, Georgia. It was founded in 1807 and was a little more than a mile long. The beautiful farmland was historically known to be the original home of the Creek Indians who over the years were displaced because of war. At the time of my birth on July 4, 1929, there were less than one hundred people living in Jacksonville.

My parents, Earlie and Maggie Darden, called me "Peas" because I was an extremely thin and small child. For years they thought I had a health problem because of my size, but my doctors proved that wasn't the case; I was just always tiny for my age. And being the only child, I received quite a bit of attention for many years.

My parents lived in a two-room flat on farmland that was owned by the man they both worked for. Daddy called him the "boss-man." Our home was nothing fancy, but what we had we kept spotless. Mom cooked and cleaned for the boss-man at the big house while Daddy worked the tobacco, cotton, and tar plantations. Daddy toiled hard all his life, and I was so proud of him. As a little girl I would watch my daddy use a metal scraper to chip tar from those large sun-loving pine trees and then gather the dark pieces in a tray he placed at the base of the trunk. When the trays were filled up, Daddy transferred the tar into large barrels. He never seemed to get tired or weary as he worked because he felt good about making an honest living and taking care of me and Mom. We were his life.

At the age of five, I was under the watchful eye of my babysitter, Cora. There were always ladies sitting around gossiping, and this day was no different. Although I was just a young child, I began to pay attention when I heard Mom's name mentioned in their conversation.

"I'm going over to her house tonight to speak to her about going off with my husband," Cora said as she looked suspiciously at the other ladies. She appeared troubled.

The conversation began to escalate as the ladies chattered back and forth while filling Cora's mind with information they heard about Mom. As Cora listened attentively, she appeared to be in deep thought. Then I remembered hearing her say, "I'm going to kill her."

Mom picked me up from the sitter's that evening, and as we were walking down the dirt road, I didn't say much. I was trying to keep up with Mom's hurried pace to get home to meet Daddy. After arriving at the house and settling in, I began to recall what I heard earlier at the babysitter's. "Cora was talking about you, Mom," I blurted out excitedly. "She said she was coming to the house tonight to kill you."

Mom looked at me in a surprised manner as if I was confused. "Go ahead, Peas, and sit down," she said sharply. "You don't know what you're talking about." She went to the kitchen to start the fire on the wood stove. She layered pieces of old, brown paper bags, a few twigs, and splinters to start the fire and then laid blocks of wood on top.

As she prepared dinner, Daddy was performing his nightly duty by starting the fireplace. He heard me speaking to my mom about what Cora said, but he never spoke a word. I sat at the table watching Daddy, longing to get up and play.

After getting the fire started, Daddy turned to me and asked, "Do you want to go out to the backyard with me and check out the chickens?"

"Yes," I answered. I immediately jumped out of my seat and followed him out the door. I loved checking on the chickens to see if they had laid eggs. I picked them up and held them like babies. I was so amused by my chickens and couldn't be happier when talking and playing with them each day. I also had the opportunity to visit my playhouse that Daddy built for me. It was one full room with a stove and table that stood right outside of the kitchen door. Mom often called out to me as I played and asked, "What are ya cooking?"

"Ham and eggs," I'd answer as I pretended to cook over the stove. I loved playing house; it was so much fun.

After collecting a few eggs that evening, Daddy and I went back into the house to wait for dinner. It wasn't too long before Mom served us at the table. I was so excited to eat because Mom made cornbread that night, and that was my favorite.

It was not long after dinner, when Mom was cleaning up the dishes, that a knock came at the door. My dad immediately got up to answer it. "Hello, Cora," he said as he opened the door. He spoke loudly as if he wanted Mom to know she was at the house.

Cora looked angry and her voice sounded somewhat abrupt. "Is Maggie home yet?" she asked.

"Yes, ma'am, she's in the kitchen washing dishes. Come on in." Daddy called out to Mom, "Maggie, Cora's here to see you." He then stepped over by the fireplace and stood watching Cora.

As Mom approached the front entrance of the house, Cora didn't waste any time with an informal greeting. She was direct and to the point.

"Maggie, where were you today?"

Mom was speechless and didn't have a chance to answer the question when Cora yelled louder, "Where were you today?" She looked furious as if the verdict was already in. "Were you off with my husband?" she asked. Cora's eyes were two times their normal size and bulging red. All of a sudden she put her hand in her coat pocket and pulled out a pistol. Then she demanded, "Maggie, answer my question. I heard you were with my husband today."

Mom stood in shock as if she didn't know where she was today. She was truly frightened and looked dumbfounded. As I listened to all the commotion, I watched the grown-ups as any child would do, trying to make sense out of what was going on. Daddy suddenly interrupted, "Wait a minute, Cora." He tried to keep a cool demeanor. "Wait a minute," he repeated. Cora frowned and began to point the pistol at Mom. "No!" she cried out in a rage, "I'm not waiting for nothing!"

Within seconds, Daddy grabbed his shotgun, which stood next to the fireplace, and he fired it over Cora's head. She yelled frantically, turned, and ran out the front door, down the hill. Mom and I practically jumped out of our skin at the sound of the gunshot.

After a few minutes of silence and shock, Daddy looked over at me with a serious look on his face. "Peas knew exactly what she was talking about," he said. "She always tells the truth."

That night and many nights to follow, Daddy and Mom fussed about everything. Sometimes it was frightening, and of course I never went back to Cora's again.

A few months went by and things began to quiet down at the house. One evening my daddy decided to attend a party at his first cousin Iman's house. Daddy was in a fairly good mood that night. He worked long hours during the week and looked forward to getting out on a Friday night to relax and wind down with family and friends.

Daddy wasn't much for dressing up. He wore his everyday clothes to go out in the evening. That night he wore blue denim overalls with a pair of tie-up brogan boots. "I'll see you later, Maggie," he hollered out and off he went.

When Daddy arrived at Iman's, the party was already in progress. The music was playing; people were dancing, laughing, and having a good time. Daddy greeted everyone with his million-dollar smile. He had pearly white teeth and loved to laugh, talk, and drink moonshine like everybody else.

Everything had seemed to be going great until the later part of the evening, when an argument broke out involving my daddy. To this day, no one knows what the argument was about. Daddy, being hotheaded, angry, and a little tipsy, left the party. He ran up the hill and back to the house. Mom and I knew something was wrong when he ran toward the fireplace, anxious to grab his shotgun.

Mom screamed out, "Earlie, what are you doin'?" Daddy ignored her. "Earlie, what are you doin'?" she repeated. "Why are you grabbing for your gun?" Daddy still refused to answer her.

He was sweating profusely as he wandered around the house with his gun in one hand and pulling open drawers with the other. He looked in closets and even under the bed. Finally he broke his silence. "Where are my bullets?" he asked. To his surprise, he found them in a box under the bed on the side where he slept.

As Daddy was on his way out of the house, he appeared to be on a mission. He had his mind made up, but Mom made a final attempt to stop him. "Please, Earlie, don't go back out there." She grabbed him by the arms to get his attention.

But Daddy, in a rage, pushed Mom out of the way and yelled, "I'll be back." Then he ran back down the hill. Mom didn't know what else to say or do. She merely shook her head in dread.

As it was told, Daddy arrived back at his cousin's house, busted open the door, and opened fire. People began screaming and running in panic. Unfortunately, Daddy accidentally shot Iman in the eye.

In that moment, Daddy knew he had done something wrong, but there was no turning back. He quickly left the scene and ran home. By the time he arrived at the house, he was out of breath and almost delirious. "Maggie, Maggie," he was distraught with fear, "I got to run! I've got to run! I shot somebody and I have to run for my life."

"What happened, Earlie?" Mom asked.

At the time, Daddy didn't know who he'd shot. He started packing a few items in a brown paper bag while Mom was trying to listen and make sense out of what he was telling her.

"Maggie, it all happened so fast," he said, "right now I have to run into the woods for a few months, and I'll return for you and Peas when everything dies down. Meanwhile, you two pack up and go stay with Grandma." Daddy gazed at Mom and me as he stood by the front door for a moment. "Maggie, I promise I'll send for you both when I get settled." His voice was trembling with regret and off he went.

Mom and I began to pack to go to Grandma's immediately after Daddy left. We took the minimum with us and left much of our belongings behind. We were somewhat fearful and didn't know what to expect, so we shared no information and gave notice to no one of our departure.

Living with Grandma was easy. I loved spending time with her but I seriously missed my daddy, even after a few days. It took about three months before Daddy sent Mom's cousin Lee in a two-door black sedan to pick us up and drive us up north to Chester, Pennsylvania. What a glorious day! I couldn't wait to see my daddy. Aunt Maude, Mom's sister, decided to relocate and travel back with us.

It was a great family reunion when we arrived to Chester. I could finally see Daddy as the car slowed down to where he stood. "There's Daddy, Mom!" I was so excited to see him. I felt butterflies in my stomach as I watched Daddy wave his hand at us, welcoming our arrival. As soon as the car stopped, I leaped out and Mom followed closely behind me. I ran into his arms and embraced him for dear life.

As for the incident back in Georgia, word came that Iman was blinded in his left eye for life from the blast. However, Daddy never talked about it again, and neither did we.

Mommy at age 9

CHAPTER 2

Move to Chester

M OM ALREADY HAD A FEW FAMILY MEMBERS living in Chester, so it was the perfect place to relocate. We initially stayed with Uncle George, Aunt Eliz, and their three children on Concord Road. It was a bit tight, but that's what families did years ago during hard times: They lived and worked together.

Aunt Maude stayed with Uncle Johnnie, her brother, and about six months later, she fell in love and married Uncle Johnnie's brother-in-law, Kent, who lived next door to them. Maude and Kent settled in a two-bedroom apartment over a garage on Flower Street. They welcomed our family to move in with them, so we did. Around this same time, Mom found a job working as a laundry woman in Ward, Pennsylvania, near Concordville. I didn't care too much for this job because Mom often stayed away from home two or three nights a week. The first time she stayed out all night, we had no idea where she was.

We didn't have telephones during those days. Therefore Daddy and I sat up all night frantic, hoping she would enter the door at any moment. When Mom finally arrived, it was the end of the next work day. She complained that she couldn't get home because she missed the last bus, so she stayed on the job.

"The Red Arrow Bus runs only twice a day," she explained, "once in the morning, then the early evening, and that's it."

Often Daddy would try to find someone to take Mom to work if she missed public transportation, but he depended on her to find a way home. If there was bad weather such as a rain- or snowstorm, Mom would not come home. "It's safer for me to stay on the job," she would argue.

Daddy didn't make too much noise about Mom staying on the job all night because he was not working yet. Besides, we needed the income, so he dealt with it.

After a few months, Daddy finally found work. Late one Saturday evening, he rushed through the front door yelling with excitement, "I got a job, Maggie, I got a job!" Daddy waited so long for this to happen and felt so relieved thanks to good ole Uncle Buddy.

Uncle Buddy was Mom's brother. He walked with a notice-able limp but never missed a day from work. Mom said when he was a boy, he climbed over a barbed wire fence, fell, and broke his leg. There were no doctors in the country town of Jacksonville during that time, so he never got treatment. His leg had to heal on its own, and he was left with a limp. "Poor folks didn't have money for doctors," Mom explained.

Mr. Alcott, Uncle Buddy's former boss, owned a moving business in Chester. He also owned and operated farmland in Concordville and a mushroom factory in West Chester. Mr. Alcott thought highly of Uncle Buddy's good reputation for work and trusted his judgment. After recommending Daddy to Mr. Alcott, he was hired at the mushroom factory.

Our family lifestyle then resembled gypsies in the sense that we moved often. It wasn't long after Daddy started working for Mr. Alcott that we relocated to a house on Springfield Valley Road in Concordville. This house was one of Mr. Alcott's properties and was located on the farm. Daddy loved this location because it was close to Mom's job and not too far from his work in West Chester.

We stayed in Concordville for about two years before relocating to a small house in Village Green. Mom managed to make our house a comfortable home wherever we lived. She worked hard inside and outside of the home.

One day she purchased about twenty-five yellow ducks from a local farmer. We kept them in a large duck coop in the back yard. It was fun to play with them every day. Mom knew I always loved ducks; they actually brought back memories of our chickens in Georgia. I will never forget chasing behind them in the yard, holding them in my arms, talking to them as my pretend friends, and helping Mom feed them each day with grain.

It was in Village Green where Mom found a new live-in job on a farm, working for Catholic nuns five days a week. The nuns allowed Mom to bring me along with her to stay in the servants' quarters attached to the convent. Our room was nothing fancy, but it was clean and comfortable. We had a bed, a dresser, and two chairs. We left Daddy at home to care for the ducks during the week, and when Mom and I returned home on weekends, we helped.

I was responsible for completing chores daily at the convent. At age six, I took pride in setting up the dining room table for breakfast, lunch, and dinner. The nuns laid me down for a nap after lunch each day, and I awoke to a variety of activities they engaged me with, including knitting and embroidery, which usually took place on the sun porch. These were very good times for me.

One weekend Cousin Lee came to pick up Daddy, Mom, and me in a two-seater car with a small crawl space in the rear. Mom and I managed to get into the crawl space while Daddy sat up front with Cousin Lee. We were going food shopping at the Great Leopard Market on Seventh and Penn Street in Chester, which was part of our routine. How we managed to get all our groceries in the car I don't know, but we did. When we finally returned home, to our surprise we found the ducks missing. We were all upset, but Mom was disgusted.

"Earlie, where are my ducks?" she cried. "Someone stole our ducks. We haven't had those ducks for even six months, and now they are gone." Mom's voice began to break up.

"I don't know where they are, but I'm going to find out," Daddy replied as he began to walk around the yard as if he was looking for clues. Daddy noticed a white neighbor looking out of her front door. "I'll be right back, Maggie," he murmured as he walked over to talk with the neighbor.

When he returned, Daddy explained to Mom that the neighbor reported "old man Bob," a white man who lived about a mile down the road, came into our yard with his pickup truck and put all the ducks in a crate and drove off. Daddy asked her if she would please call the sheriff, and she did.

It wasn't long afterward when the patrol car drove up to the house and Daddy walked over to meet the sheriff. "How can I help you folks?" he asked Daddy with a serious and stern look. Daddy nervously explained what the neighbor told him. The sheriff never looked directly at my daddy but appeared to be listening. Almost cutting him off, he said, "Okay, let's go check it out." He returned to his patrol car, and Daddy followed him. Daddy sat in the back seat of the patrol car, and off they went down the road.

Mom was confident that they had a case because the incident was eye witnessed by the neighbor. However, when the patrol car returned within the hour, Daddy got out looking very disappointed. "What happened, Earlie?" Mom asked.

Daddy started to respond, but the sheriff spoke up. "I'm sorry, Earlie, but you heard him. Bob said the ducks belong to him. He paid for them and takes good care of the ducks in his yard. He doesn't know what happened to your ducks. I'm sorry," he said.

"But my wife brought those ducks from the city market,"

Daddy responded. "Plus the neighbor saw Mr. Bob taking them out of our yard. Don't that count for something?"

"I'm sorry, nothing I can do," the sheriff said. "It's your word against his." He returned to his patrol car and slowly drove off. Mom and Daddy looked so disappointed and hurt. Shortly after that incident, we moved back to Chester.

Daddy found a rooming house on Central Avenue. Unfortunately, Mom could no longer work for the nuns because there was no means of transportation and Daddy wanted her home. I started first grade at Perry Wright School while Daddy started another job doing seasonal construction work. These were hard times for our family, but it was a time of economic depression for many folks back then. Roosevelt was president at the time, World War II was in progress, and the unexpected bombing against the United States naval base at Pearl Harbor happened in 1941.

Around 1945 things began to change for Daddy. The job market opened up, and he found work at Sun Shipbuilding and Dry Dock Company in Chester as a chipper. Daddy said this was a real job, and now he could save money with the idea of getting us a house.

One day Daddy came home from work in a cheerful mood. He was smiling as he called out to Mom, "Maggie come here, I want to take you somewhere and show you something."

"Okay, okay," Mom replied, trying to figure out what was going on.

Daddy pulled her by the arm, and she followed. They left the house walking toward Tenth and Edward Street when finally after a few blocks, Daddy stopped and pointed to a large house. "I want to get this for us," he said.

Mom couldn't believe her eyes. It seemed like a mini-mansion. Daddy already had the keys from the rental agent, so they were able to enter the house. Mom and Daddy were excited about the house as they went from room to room, inspecting every nook, crack, and cranny. It had about ten rooms with plenty of space, and Mom loved it. That was the deciding factor for Daddy, and he didn't waste any time securing the property with a deposit to the landlord.

It was only a matter of days before we began to pack up our belongings and move into our new home. Daddy also allowed many of Mom's family members to live with us—those who needed a room. He felt proud to be able to help someone in need of housing because he had been assisted so many times before.

I transferred to a new school for second grade called Booker T. Washington and remained there until sixth grade when I was promoted to Douglas Junior High School. Mom made sure I was one of the best-dressed children in school. Being the only child, I always had the newest-style clothes and shoes. Mom took pride in how I went out in public, and I often got compliments from adults on my appearance. Yet I must admit that school was often a struggle for me. From the time I started church school back in Georgia at age five, I had problems socializing with other children. You might say I always had an assigned bully all throughout my school years. It never bothered me to move or change schools because I was always hoping things would get better, but that never happened. It was hard for me to make new friends, I didn't like to study, and I always felt different or out of place. Girls would pick on me for any reason or none at all. They called me skinny, stole my lunch, and one day they threw rocks at me just for fun and games. I was always quiet and tried everything to avoid troublemakers, but it didn't help.

I told my mom one day that a girl was stealing pickles from my lunch. Mom talked with me and cautioned me to be careful, but nothing else came out of it. So I pretty much kept most things to myself because I thought it was senseless to share what I was going through in school since nothing helped. Year after year my dislike for school grew greater, and my parents knew it.

The final incident I encountered was in tenth grade. I had a Spanish teacher named Mr. Hill. One day I was out sick and on my return to class, he confronted me with a question in Spanish, "¿Has hecho los deberes?"

"What?" I responded. "I don't understand what you're saying."

"Did you do your homework?" he asked in an abrupt tone.

"What homework? I was out sick."

He walked over to my desk and punched my back with his fist clenched and walked away. I was in shock and didn't move. It embarrassed me while the other kids looked on in amusement. Some even laughed. I barely made it through school on that day; I had been humiliated. When I finally arrived home, I tearfully informed Daddy of what happened in school, and for the first time he became very angry.

"Mr. Hill punched you in the back?" he asked as if he didn't hear what I said.

"Yes, Daddy, and everybody laughed," I answered.

"What is going on at that school? I'll see him tomorrow and see if he punches me. I'm sick and tired of these schools. Do you hear me Peas? I'll be going up to that school first thing in the morning," Daddy said, trying to comfort me. "I will talk to the principal and then see Mr. Hill," he promised.

In all fairness, Cousin Fannie warned me not to sign up to take Spanish with Mr. Hill because, as she said, he had a violent temper. I totally ignored her because I had such a curiosity and deep desire to speak Spanish as a second language.

The very next day, Daddy kept his word and came up to the school. Mr. Valentine, the principal, called Daddy into his office, and I was sent to class. Daddy explained everything that I had told him. Mr. Valentine listened very carefully and never rushed Daddy. When it was his turn to respond to the complaint, however, he began to speak up for the teacher.

"Mr. Hill is one of the best teachers in this school. I will investigate what happened and get back to you. Perhaps there is some misunderstanding," he said.

"I believe my daughter," Daddy exclaimed. "She has no reason to lie." After about twenty minutes, Daddy left Mr. Valentine's office feeling somewhat dissatisfied because he never had the opportunity to talk with the teacher directly.

When I arrived home, Daddy appeared disappointed and angry. "Peas, you don't have to put up with those teachers anymore," he said as he looked me directly in the eyes and put his hand on my shoulder to ensure that I was listening, "You are not going back to that school."

I was startled and yet relieved. I dropped out of school in the tenth grade and never looked back. With the extra time at home, I signed up for a home correspondence course in an attempt to complete high school by mail, but after several months I lost interest.

"Maggie, it's time!" Daddy announced to Mom as he walked into the kitchen. Mom was busy preparing dinner.

"Time for what?" Mom asked. She looked puzzled.

"It's time for us to buy our own home. I believe I found a small house at Eleventh and Edward Street that we can call our own. No more moving from place to place," he said. Daddy had managed to save five hundred dollars. A real estate agent had told him this was enough to get the house he wanted. It was just a matter of time and paperwork before my daddy would achieve the American dream of home ownership.

After a few months, it became a reality when our family celebrated the move into our new home on Eleventh and Edward Street on a cold rainy day. This was the family trio's final move together and where we planted a stake in the ground.

CHAPTER 3

Major Milestone

"MOM, I'M HOME" I CALLED OUT AS I ENTERED the front door. The lights were dim and the house was quiet. "Mom!" I said, this time shouting a little louder, but still there was no response. *Where's Mom?* I wondered. I was excited to tell her about my day in school, so I ran throughout the house but found no one. The furniture was in place, the throw rugs lay properly, and the heavy lace curtains at the windows were flowing as usual, but something was different. I felt it in my gut. I continued through the house toward the kitchen, where I usually met Mom—in the kitchen cooking supper. Supper time was the hour when Mom and I would get together and discuss our day. This was our girl time together. *Oh well, maybe she ran out to the store*, I thought. I opened the ice box, got something to drink, and went into the dining room, where I noticed a note on the table with some money. *What's this?* I asked myself.

Dear Peas,

I'm going away. Can't explain it to you now.
Here is the money for school. I'll be in touch.

Mom

That simple note with few words left me confused. What did she mean by "going away?" Going away to where? Be in touch when? I was eighteen years old then, but that day I felt like I was eight. I literally went into shock! I didn't know what to think. I could not process what she was saying in the note. I decided to wait until Daddy came home. Maybe he could explain the note. I headed to my bedroom to wait.

I had always lived a pretty normal life for a "Georgia peach." That's what they called a young lady from Georgia. My parents married at a very young age, and as their only daughter, I felt confident about their love for me. I often longed to share my life with a brother or sister however being an only child has its advantages. We were a poor working-class family like everybody else in the neighborhood, yet my needs were always met.

Reaching the age of eighteen was a major milestone for me because I was now considered an adult, capable of making my own decisions about my life. I had the opportunity to enroll in an LPN nursing program out of Philadelphia despite my tenth grade dropout status. I felt really proud about doing something new and different with my life. My desire to be unique from other girls in my community inspired me to want more for myself. My parents supported my dreams to become a nurse even though they never pushed me to complete high school. Of course back in my parents' day, it was a different time. A person could still make a good living without finishing high school. That neither of them completed school made it easy for them to accept my strong dislike for school and to drop out. Yet on this beautiful autumn day, I arrived home from nursing school excited about my life and ready to share with the world what I learned, but no one was there.

I heard Daddy when he finally arrived home and ran down to meet him. I immediately gave him the note, which was still lying on the dining room table. "What's this?" he asked.

"Read it, Daddy," I replied.

Daddy started cursing Mom and calling her every name in the book but a child of God. "I'm going to kill Clayton!" he yelled over and over. "I'm going to kill him! I'm going to kill Clayton!" Daddy acted as if he knew what was behind the note.

Clayton was the man who came to stay with us a few months earlier. Daddy found him sleeping on Aunt Suzy's couch next door. The word out on him was he came up to Chester from the south, trying to find his wife. Apparently she had run off because he tried to kill her by busting her in the head with an oil lamp. Clayton currently had no job and was down on his luck. Of course my daddy felt sorry for him, and the two became friends, started hanging out, and eventually Daddy took him into our home. I personally never felt good about Clayton. There was something about him that I didn't like. He stayed with us for less than six months, and the entire time I was suspicious of him—for what, I didn't know.

Once I came home from school and found all the doors locked, which was unusual. I knocked and yelled for Mom almost ten minutes before she finally opened the door. There Clayton was, sitting on the couch in the living room with a strange look on his face. "Mom, what took you so long to open the door?" I asked.

Mom could barely look at me when she answered in a whisper, "Peas, I didn't hear the door." She quickly changed the subject. "How was school?" As I began to talk to Mom about my day in school, I dismissed the incident.

As Daddy continued to stare at the note, he took a seat at the table. He read the note over and over again as if some new information would become visible. The woman he loved, the mother of his only child, had walked out on him. It made no sense! He looked as if he had lost his best friend; he was so hurt. He appeared to be in deep thought while perspiration poured down on his face.

"Peas, if it's the last thing I do, I am going to kill him," he said. I tried to comfort Daddy by rubbing his back, but I was in a state of shock myself. Daddy looked me shamefully in the eyes. "Peas, I put him out of the house because I found out that him and your mom was having an affair." Tears began to break through from his eyes, and he dropped his face into his hands.

There was much silence in the house that night, and for me a list of unanswered questions. My Mom and I were so close.

Why didn't she tell me she had plans to leave? I never saw any signs that she would leave me and Daddy. I felt so emotionally confused that I cried all night. Days and weeks went by, and I heard no word about mom. I literally slipped into a state of depression that made it impossible for me to concentrate in school. I had difficulty sleeping at night and cried so often that I was almost tearless. My father could barely console me because he was so bitter and distraught himself.

Months went by, and there still was no word about Mom from family or friends. Daddy and I didn't know if she was living or dead. I began to turn to my boyfriend Willis for comfort. He was such a good friend—we had been dating for almost a year and a half. I cared a lot about Willis and hoped to marry him someday. At least that was my dream. One night, on Christmas Eve, we were walking home from a dance holding hands when Willis began to tell me that he had a surprise for me and wanted to ask me something.

"What is it?" I asked him. My mind began to race with the idea of marriage. *This is it!* I thought to myself, *He will ask to marry me.*

"I don't know how to ask you," he answered.

"Ask me what?" I responded. He paused for a few minutes and then blurted out, "I want us to shack together."

My face expression dropped! "What?" I asked again as if I didn't hear him the first time.

"I want us to shack up ... you know ... live together," he explained.

I was speechless and not that kind of girl. What was he thinking about me all this time we had been dating? I was almost voiceless but managed to speak as calmly and firmly as I could: "If I'm not good enough for you to marry, then I'm not good enough for you to sleep with." I immediately broke hands with him and said angrily, "What kind of girl do you think I am, Willis?" I walked away from Willis that night, ran home, and cried all night. I never heard from him again.

The sudden breakup did not help my state of mind. Losing both my mom and my boyfriend in a matter of months was too much for me. This downhill spiral of broken and lost relationships caused a great turning point in my life. I began to read my Bible in search of God. I looked for a supernatural intervention. I needed God to console me.

The New Year had arrived with still no word about Mom. I did, however, run into Willis' sister Margaret one day as I was walking to church.

"Did you hear the news?" she asked.

"What news?" I responded.

"Willis ran off with a married woman and is living with her in another state."

My mouth dropped opened and my eyes almost popped out of my head. I was stunned! Here I thought Willis cared so much about me. What a phony! Margaret watched my reaction as I shook my head in disgust. I remained speechless and slowly walked away from the conversation.

Just a few days later, I received a letter from Grandma, who was still living in Hazlehurst, Georgia. She wrote:

Peas,

I found out where your mom is staying.
Please come to Hazlehurst as soon as you can,
and we will take you to her.

Grandma

I screamed! "Daddy, Daddy, they found Mom!" All through the house I screamed for joy! Finally, my eyes became bright and hopeful. I laughed, then danced and thanked God. I cried—but this time it was tears of joy. This news was a light at the end of a dark tunnel that I had been living in for several months. "Thank God! My prayers were answered."

I began to pack and make travel arrangements immediately even though it would take a few more weeks to get the money from Daddy in order to go. He had no desire to go to Georgia but knew it was important for me to go, and he supported me in that. Daddy was still battling his anger and hurt feelings about Mom. He never really talked about her coming back to him, but I do believe he loved her. My daddy's heart and spirit took a big hit when Mom left us. Although he was a strong man, he was broken over the loss of his wife.

CHAPTER 4

Back to Georgia

I T WAS A FEW DAYS BEFORE EASTER SUNDAY WHEN
I finally took the train to Georgia. It seemed like an unusually long ride. I was excited about traveling, but I also felt a little anxious and nervous about the unknown. I kept thinking about what I wanted to say to Mom and what she would say to me.

After I arrived in Hazlehurst and settled in at Grandma's house, she began to tell me how she found Mom. "Your Uncle Tommy and Uncle Bubba was out partying around town and ran into Clayton. He and your mom are living out in Lumber City." Grandma wasted no time telling me everything I needed to know to find Mom. Within a few days, with the help of Uncle Bubba, I was on my way to Lumber City, carrying a small bag of my belongings.

As we drove down miles of dirt road in Lumber City, I found a shack straight ahead with the address that I was looking for. Was this where Clayton lived? To my surprise, a woman was standing in the doorway. *Is that Mom?* I asked myself. Uncle Bubba dropped me off near the place and left. As I slowly approached the shack, I realized it *was* Mom! Fear gripped me as I came near her and glanced shyly into her eyes. Mom looked so sad and starting crying when she realized it was me. She appeared embarrassed, and I noticed immediately that she had gained a considerable amount of weight around her stomach. Her skin also appeared darker, she had plaits in her hair, and she wore an old cotton dress. I couldn't believe my eyes.

"Hi Mom," I said. "I didn't know where you were, and Daddy's all upset!"

It was an awkward moment. I became teary-eyed, but after Mom reached out to me, I felt relieved. "Come on inside," Mom replied as she led the way into her place.

The shack where Mom lived was considered a bungalow and servant's quarter for a large tobacco plantation. It sat on bricks to hold it above ground, and there were wood shutters for windows. Inside were three rooms—a bedroom, a living room, and a kitchen. I noticed a wood stove in the kitchen area, with a wood table and a few old wooden chairs. A couch was positioned in the living room, but there were no other decorations or pictures to beautify the residence. The outhouse was located just a few feet away from the main house, and it resembled a small wooden house the size of a telephone booth with a hole in the dirt ground. The hole was surrounded by a raised wooden bench with an opening in it. I was fearful of using outhouses mainly because a close relative found a snake in the hole while using one, and it frightened her to death.

Clayton earned his right to live here by farming and toiling acres and acres of tobacco plants that surrounded an absolutely beautiful mansion further down the road.

I had such a peace in my spirit after reuniting with Mom. I stayed with her for about two weeks but never took my stuff out of my bags. Clayton never allowed me to feel "right at home." Of course he never said anything to me that would make me feel this way, but he made subtle gestures. His politeness toward me was as phony as a three-dollar bill. This man broke up my family, and I really didn't care for him at all. My main concern was for my mom.

One night I overheard Mom vomiting in her bedroom while I laid in my bed. I dared not go into her room while Clayton was in there, so I listened carefully. Mom gagged and hacked for a little while, but after it became quiet, I feel off to sleep.

Mom made it through the night. The next day she got up early to get dressed. "Peas, I'm going to the doctor's office because I felt sick last night," she said.

"Okay," I responded without making any other comments.

Mom and Clayton walked about a mile to the doctor's office while I stayed at the house. Once they returned, I anxiously asked Mom what the doctor had to say.

Mom looked sadly and regrettably into my eyes and said, "The doctor said he thinks I got a tumor in my stomach."

I was speechless! "Ohh." I asked no questions at the time

because I really didn't want to talk in front of Clayton. I was deeply concerned about Mom because I had never seen her sick before. Everything was so different, so I decided to go back to Grandma's in Hazlehurst to let her know what was going on.

"She didn't look good at all," I reported to Grandma as we sat and talked about my visit to Mom's.

"I'm so sorry, Peas, I don't know what has come over my child." Grandma looked so grieved over the news. We sat for a while to comfort each other.

My thoughts were to help Mom get out of that situation before I fully understood what her desires were. I began to pursue employment so that I could be in a position to assist her. While looking for work, one day I met a man named Luis. He delivered ice in the community, and I shared with him my desire to find a job. He mentioned he had a cousin named Inez who knew a lot of people around town and could probably help me find a job.

Luis was a tall, handsome man with olive-colored skin, curly hair, and brown eyes that could hypnotize. He was a fine dresser and drove a four-door black Plymouth car. Luis was very active in the civil rights movement; he was a key person in getting many petitions signed for colored people to get the legal right to vote. And he was such a gentleman!

Luis brought Inez around to Grandma's house one evening just to introduce her to me. He seemed concerned about my situation and wanted to help me.

Inez and I hit it off right away. She was a pleasant and friendly young woman. I noticed right away that she enjoyed laughing. She smiled often as if waiting to burst into laughter at any moment. During our conversation that night, Inez informed me that there were two doctors in Telfair County, and she worked for one of them. "His name is Dr. Youma, and he is a general practitioner," she said. Apparently she had cooked for Dr. Youma for quite some time, but said that she had plans to leave. "I will be glad to introduce you to him if you like."

"Okay. I would love to meet him." I felt this was a sure lead to a new job, which I so desperately needed.

A few days later, I visited Inez at her home where I found out that she was married, had two children, and loved to cook.

That same day, Inez took me to her place of employment and introduced me to Dr. Youma and his wife. They were a middle-aged Southern couple with one school-age daughter. They both took a liking to me almost instantly. "Ohh ... a little Yankee," Dr. Youma teased in his Southern accent, "I think I will hire her in your place, and each summer she can go with my wife and daughter to Saint Simon Island." He first looked at Inez and then turned to me. "Would you like that?"

"Yes sir," I replied. I was thrilled to have my first job offer in Georgia come from a doctor. Feeling eager to let Mom know that I was hired as a cook and mother's helper, I immediately made plans to visit Lumber City. I also showed gratitude to Inez for all her help in preparing me for the job.

To my surprise, Mom and Clayton came to visit us before I had the opportunity to get to Lumber City. Mom and I were elated to see each other and began to catch up on what was happening. She was excited about my new job and my plans to help her financially. In turn, I found out that she and Clayton were making plans to move to Hazlehurst. Mom insisted that I should move in with them, and of course I agreed despite my feelings about her boyfriend. She also mentioned that Clayton was having problems with his boss on the tobacco farm and was looking for a new job.

I noticed Mom's abdomen looking larger than before, yet she failed to talk about her health issues during our conversation, so I asked, "Mom what is the doctor saying about the tumor?"

"I'm feeling so much better, Peas," she answered, "all of that is under control." Mom quickly and firmly changed the subject, so I dared not tread on that topic any longer.

Upon completing my first week with Dr. Youma, he gave me a total of ten dollars in wages. I used this money to help Grandma around the house, but everything after that week went to Mom's new place. I paid for rent and food; I purchased a new couch, a kitchen table with chairs, and bed linens from the general store. I set up an agreement with the store manager to make payments on the items every two weeks until it was paid off. Everything was delivered and set up to my liking, which made it even more exciting to move.

Finally, I gathered all my belongings from Grandma's, made the move, and settled in. The new place was a bungalow and had the same setup as the shack in Lumber City: two rooms and a kitchen.

"Peas, I have something I want to tell you," Mom said as we sat at the kitchen table one evening after supper.

"Today I had an appointment to see my new doctor in Hazlehurst, and he said I'm pregnant. I didn't know the right time to tell you." The sound of her voice was apologetic.

Speechless for a moment, I then asked, "Did you ever have a tumor?"

"No, Peas, I don't have a tumor." Mom repeated as gently as she could: "I'm pregnant." She stared at me to watch my facial expression, knowing that I would be disappointed, then continued: "I was too ashamed to tell you or your dad. That's why I left Chester the way I did."

"How many months are you, Mom?" I responded. "Does Clayton know?"

"Yeah, he knows. I'm pretty far gone now. Isn't anything I can do about it."

I didn't know how Clayton felt about the pregnancy because he and Mom didn't get along that well from what I could see. Now that he wasn't working, Clayton was drinking more, sometimes staying out all night, and becoming increasingly mean to Mom. Not only was he verbally abusive toward Mom at times, but one night I overheard him talking loudly about me, knowing that I was right in the next room. Mom tried to quiet him down when he yelled, "Who the hell is Peas?"

At least my question had been answered as to why Mom ran off from home. It had nothing to do with me or Daddy but rather her own weakness. I believe Mom knew her time was close to delivering the baby, and she had to share her secret with me. We talked for a while that evening, and I eventually began to feel good about having a little brother or sister.

It was less than two weeks later when a midwife came to visit us at the house, and Mom gave birth to a beautiful six-pound baby girl named Ann. I still found it hard to believe that despite my age, it never registered in my mind that Mom was pregnant. I must have been green as grass! She was seven months pregnant when I first found her and she had been too ashamed to confess her sins.

I had been working for Dr. Youma for a few months when the word spread throughout town that Inez had been murdered. Apparently she was having an affair with a married man, and his wife found out. One evening the wife secretly trailed her husband and Inez into the woods when she found them in his car naked and making out. The wife took out a gun, went up to the car window, and shot Inez point blank in the head. She died instantly, but the husband was able to run away from the scene.

Working for Dr. Youma gave me the opportunity to meet many interesting people. One day on my way to work, I stopped by the medical office to pick up my pay. While there I met a Catholic nun in the waiting room; she was scheduled for a checkup with the doctor. I immediately noticed her pleasant and friendly demeanor towards me as she began to converse about her recent move to the area with three other nuns to establish a convent. This would be the first convent in Hazlehurst, and she appeared very excited about it.

I informed her of my cooking abilities when she put me to the test. "Can you make me an apple pie?" she asked. "Sure can!" I replied, "apple pies are my specialty." We then made plans to meet at the office within a few days so I could deliver the pie to her. It was because of this interaction that I even contemplated becoming a nun. I felt these women lived sacred lives dedicated to God and serving people. This in turn inspired me.

Doctor Youma spoke highly of my work, and my name began to get around town, which led to several job offers. I managed to take on a second job, working for Dr. Martin as a part-time cook. This was a temporary assignment because I filled in for someone who had been out on sick leave. Still, in this short period I was able to save a good sum of money as I made between eight and ten dollars a week.

I landed another job with the sheriff of Hazlehurst and stayed only a few months because I desired higher wages. Finally I was offered a cooking job with a multimillionaire named Mr. Cook, who was part owner of General Motors in Chicago. He paid a little more than the other jobs, and I was happy to work for him.

My daily schedule consisted of cooking for Dr. Youma in the morning until about 12:30 p.m., then walking across town to work for Mr. Cook. He lived in a beautiful landscaped mansion and employed many workers that kept his land up.

I loved to work because my jobs were so fulfilling—they

gave me purpose. I always felt good about being independent, having my own money, and having the ability to help others.

As Ann began to grow and develop in speech, Clayton taught her to curse Mom out. To complicate matters even worse, Clayton moved his nine-year-old son Rudy into our home and Mom announced she was pregnant once again.

Little Rudy was a handful! He felt he did not have to listen to Mom and showed little respect for her. I believe he saw the way Clayton treated Mom and followed his father's lead. One day little Rudy told a big lie about Mom. He informed Clayton that Mom was doing more for me and less for him, which made Clayton extremely angry.

"I will kill you if you ever mistreat my son," he yelled. Clayton was abusive and meant every word he said. I felt Mom's pain because he had a violent temper and threatened her on several occasions. Mom was quiet and would not respond to avoid making matters worse.

I knew Clayton was not happy about this pregnancy because he showed it in the way he treated Mom. Their relationship was deteriorating fast.

With so much stress and pressure on Mom during this pregnancy, she began to have complications. Her blood pressure became extremely high and a cause for worry. One day the visiting midwife was examining Mom and called for the doctor that I worked for. When Dr. Youma arrived, he worked hard to deliver the baby, but it was a stillborn birth.

Once again Clayton decided to move the family, but this

time I stayed behind. I knew he didn't like me and believed he was happy to leave me behind. The relationship between him and Mom was the same—abusive and destructive, but that was Mom's life and not mine. She chose that for herself.

A few weeks after their move, Mom walked almost two miles with Ann to come visit me. She appeared to be at an all-time low.

"I got to get away from him, Peas. I can't take any more," Mom said. She looked depressed, and for the first time I heard her talk about leaving Clayton. I believe this was a turning point for her, and she finally came to her senses.

"What are you going to do, Mom? Will you go back to Grandma's?" I was so glad that she planned to leave Clayton.

"I can't go back to Grandma's because she's planning to move up north with Leroy."

Grandma had finally submitted to Leroy's request to move in with him in Chester. He had plenty of room to accommodate her. He lived in a house with an attached garage that he had renovated into a kitchen and bedroom. This is where Grandma would stay.

I would miss Grandma, but lately I understood that life's situations and circumstances change, and we have to be able to adjust even when those changes are hurtful.

Although Mom was dreadfully afraid of Clayton, she secretly began making plans to leave him, and of course I supported her. She also planned to move back to Chester and stay with members of her family because this would be a safe haven for her. Finally, Mom got up the courage to set a date for her departure.

Clayton left for work as usual one morning, and Mom quickly packed a few things for herself and Ann to travel with on the train. I met Mom at her place, and wasting no time, we walked as fast as we could to the Hazlehurst train station where I purchased the tickets. Mom was scheduled to change trains once she reached Macon that afternoon. As we waited in the Hazlehurst station, I saw one of Clayton's friends but turned my head quickly and cautioned Mom about him. I realized that he recognized us and began to watch us carefully. We stood quietly and totally ignored him as if we never saw him. Finally the train arrived, and I hung around until I saw Mom board the train with little Ann. I felt so relieved when I caught Mom's eye as she waved goodbye to me from the window. She was finally free from Clayton I thought.

After leaving the train station, and on my way for a dentist appointment, I began to think about everything: my dad back home, Mom, little Ann, Clayton, my job, and even that day's upcoming visit to the dentist to get two teeth pulled.

I also thought about Luis. I was beginning to have deep feelings for him. From the first time I met him near Grandma's place, I knew there was something special about him. I loved his company, and the more time I spent with him, the more my feelings grew. I also became close to his family. He had five sisters and one brother. His sisters and I went shopping together, attended tennis tournaments, and church almost on a regular basis.

Each day I was so excited to see Luis. We went out about three times a week, and with everything going on in my life, he was a great relief for me. We visited the local café one evening and sat in the car for hours just talking to each other. He often discussed his activities with the civil rights movement. Luis would go door to door at night to get signatures to win the opportunity for blacks to vote. He was passionate about the advancement of our community. Luis was a Methodist man, and I prayed one day he would be my husband.

"Why did I get two teeth pulled at one time?" I thought out loud as I sat in the dentist's chair after the extractions. Everything went well, but I had a terrible headache afterward. When I arrived home, I immediately went straight to my bed for rest. I was worn out from the day's activities and needed to recuperate for work the next day. I fell off to sleep, and just a few hours later as I lay in my bed, lo and behold, I heard someone coming in the kitchen door. When I looked up, who did I see but Mom and Ann? At first I thought I was hallucinating. "What happened?" I cried almost shouting.

"Peas, Clayton met us in Macon. When we changed trains, he was already at the station waiting," she said, teary-eyed. Mom was easygoing and very fearful of Clayton, so she never argued or attempted to fight back.

I had hoped and prayed that by the time the news got back to Clayton, Mom and Ann would be long gone from Georgia.

Unfortunately, Clayton's friend, being suspicious of Mom and me, connected with Clayton as soon as he left the station in Hazlehurst.

When Mom and Ann first got off the train in Macon, they did not notice Clayton. As they stood on the platform, waiting for the next train heading north, Clayton walked briskly up to them, snatched Ann from Mom, and ran off. Mom, tearful and in shock, ran after him and reluctantly went back home because she refused to leave without Ann. Clayton later informed Mom that as soon as he found out about the train heading for Macon, he immediately paid a taxicab to take him to the train station. While I listened to Mom explain what happened, she looked pitiful. I was disappointed and felt bad for her.

That July, my schedule included traveling with Mrs. Youma and her daughter, Cindy. They vacationed at their summer cottage on Saint Simons Island, a beautiful place for a refreshing vacation. I cooked for the family. Mrs. Youma and Cindy enjoyed the amusement park, walking the boardwalk, and relaxing on the beach each year. Dr. Youma would join them some weekends when he was not working.

I prepared breakfast, lunch, and dinner at the cottage while Mrs. Youma and Cindy made their way to the boardwalk to engage in a variety of activities each day and returning to the cottage for meals. One of my favorite recipes they enjoyed was my hush puppies. I cooked them with fish on several nights, and they raved about them.

As the vacation came to an end on a Saturday evening and

we arrived back home, I began to prepare my clothes for church the next day. I was a junior missionary, worked with youth, and sang in the choir. I was also called on frequently to read condolences at various funerals. Mrs. Youma knew of my involvement with my church, and she encouraged me in it. She once nominated me to win a scholarship to attend Camp Hope in Augusta, Georgia, for two weeks, sponsored by the white Methodist church. To my surprise, I was chosen to attend, and while there I met many young girls from different counties in Georgia. We had so much fun as well as plenty of food and fellowship. We played a variety of games and learned to sing many new songs. One of the songs, "Have Thine Own Way," continued to ring in my heart long after the trip and is still one of my favorite songs today.

The trip to Camp Hope was a great opportunity for me, one that certainly taught me a lot. After returning home, I was called to speak at the white Methodist church to give a report about my two weeks at the camp. This event was the first time any colored people had been invited, and I was more than happy to go.

I loved attending church and being involved in the activities offered. In addition to working on the job, church was a major part of my life. This was true for many colored people back then. Church was a vehicle for community fellowship, support, spiritual maturity and personal growth.

Mr. Cook, my boss, came to visit my church quite frequently on Sunday evenings. I often noticed him sitting on the back pew, clapping his hands, and shaking his head while enjoying the gospel music. He showed his genuine commitment to the four colored churches in our community when he donated five hundred dollars to each church.

It was well known that he cared about colored people. I recall a house fire in my neighborhood from an oil burner explosion, causing a little colored girl to have third degree burns to over seventy-five percent of her body. Mr. Cook intervened. He paid for the ambulance service to take her to a special burn center in Atlanta and also included expenses for the family to travel with her because they couldn't afford to pay. In my eyes Mr. Cook was a great man.

To my surprise, I received a telegram from Aunt Mary (Mom's sister) up north saying that Grandma had passed away. Apparently she had been outside in the yard chopping wood in dry heat, suffered a stroke, and died in the yard. Grandma never wanted to be buried in Pennsylvania and made that known. Therefore the family desired for her body to return to Georgia to be buried with her own people. Unfortunately, money was an issue. I shared the information with the only person who I believed would help me, Mr. Cook. After explaining the situation to him, he generously offered to pay all expenses to get Grandma's body back to Georgia. What a relief! My family was so happy to be able to grant Grandma's final wish.

Since most of the family was up north, they had a small service for Grandma at Hunt's Funeral Home in Chester, and then she was transported to Georgia by train. Mr. Cook had arranged for the colored undertaker in Georgia to pick up the body once it arrived and make the necessary arrangements for burial. As planned, the undertaker was ready and waiting with flowers as the train pulled into the station. Grandma was buried the next day.

Mom and I did not view her body but chose to remember her as she was—a woman filled with so much life! Thanks to God and Mr. Cook, it all worked out.

By then I had been living in Georgia for almost five years and began to reflect on what was going on in my personal life. I wanted to see some changes. First, I found myself madly in love with Luis. We were still dating, and I dreamed that he would one day be my husband. He was such a great support to me. However, he had not hinted to me even once about marriage. We enjoyed each other's company, but where were we going?

I also really desired to see things change for Mom. Now that Clayton knew she was trying to get away from him, he became more protective and suspicious of anything she did. He was an angry man and did not want her to have any involvement with me nor any of the family. Mom still managed to communicate with me by sneaking over to visit while Clayton was working. She and I continued to talk about making changes in her living arrangements and believed one day she would get away from him. She was not happy, and she literally feared Clayton.

Finally we devised a plan. One night when Clayton was out, Mom quickly walked to my place with little Ann, and I arranged for Luis to meet us there. Luis drove us to West Green where Mom stayed with Uncle Tommie, her brother. This was a safe place for her because Clayton did not know where Uncle Tommie lived, and she could hide out here until it was safe for her to travel back north. I am not sure if Clayton tried to search for Mom this time because neither I nor Mom ever heard from him or mentioned his name again.

Early one Sunday morning a few weeks later, I arrived at work to find a telegram from Aunt Mary on the electric range. The telegram read: "Come immediately, your dad has had a stroke."

Dr. Youma also wrote a second note: "We're at church, and will try to get back before you leave, but cook what you have to cook."

I was so surprised that I was almost paralyzed and could hardly cook. Upon thinking deeply about it, I realized I had to leave Georgia. My dad needed me now more than ever. For the previous five years, living in Georgia had filled an important part of my life. Finding my mom, the job opportunities that were offered to me here, and my relationship with Luis were all dear to my heart. Now the time had come for a change.

When the Youma family arrived home from church, they showed much compassion toward me. Dr. Youma gave me two hundred dollars cash, and Mrs. Youma baked a chocolate cake with white frosting for me to take on the road. They both wished me the best, and I left work early that day, unsure if I would ever return.

Luis and I met faithfully each Sunday afternoon, and I could hardly wait to see him. There were not many telephones back then, so calling was not an option for poor folks. While waiting for Luis at the house, I packed and organized my belongings until he finally arrived. I explained the telegram about Daddy and my short day at work.

"What are you going to do?" he asked.

"I'm going home," I responded with much regret. "I have to go and take care of Daddy. He needs me."

"What about your mom?"

"I want Mom to go with me. She's planning to move back north anyway, and now would be the perfect time. We could probably go together." By then I was anxious to see Mom and let her know what was going on. "Would you take me to West Green to tell her?" I asked.

"Yell any time you want to go," he answered. Luis never hesitated to help me, so off we went that same afternoon.

It took about an hour and a half to drive to West Green, but I felt at peace being side-by-side with Luis in the car. When we arrived, I met Mom inside the house. She instantly knew something was wrong before I could even speak.

"What's wrong, Peas?" she asked.

"Daddy had a stroke and he's in the hospital," I said. "Mom, I'm going back home to be with him. Will you come with me?"

Mom was surprised at the news but wasn't sure if she wanted to return north with me because of the circumstances involved in her leaving. However, Uncle Tommy talked her into going back with me because he felt it was the right thing to do. Besides, she shouldn't have ever been in Georgia in the first place. So we made plans to leave together.

As Luis and I returned home that late evening, it was quiet in the car. Each moment it became more apparent that we had to part from each other for a little while at least, and I felt emotionally saddened. I loved Luis and desired to be with him forever.

Luis parked the car and walked me to the door. Appearing very serious, he looked me directly in the eyes and said, "Peas, I want to say this to you. I care a lot about you ... but when you get back north, if you should happen to meet someone else, I don't want to hold you back. I'm not ready for anything serious right now."

My mouth dropped. I was so shocked! After all these years of being together, I thought we were closer than that. I felt broken at this point. I thought I would hear words of a more serious nature, possibly about marriage. Instead I heard words promoting closure. It's so hard to believe that I suddenly face leaving Georgia, my job and my beloved boyfriend.

A few days later, Luis picked me up, and we were on our way to West Green once again to pick up Mom and Ann. As I sat quietly in the car, I thought much about parting with Luis, and I didn't feel good about it. I really loved him and could not imagine our relationship was pretty much over.

We were headed to Lumber City for the 9 p.m. evening train headed north and were scheduled to change in Macon and once again in Atlanta. I was so relieved that Mom and Ann were going back with me, but it didn't erase the hurt and disappointment I felt about leaving Luis. Still, it was good to travel with my family as we made our way back home.

CHAPTER 5

Relocating Back to Pennsylvania

THE TRAIN RIDE TO CHESTER SEEMED FOREVER. I had such a headache, which made it impossible to rest during the ride. Finally pulling into the Chester station, we saw Uncle Kent standing on the platform and waiting. Mom, Ann, and I were more than happy to finally exit the train. We made plans to stay with Uncle Kent and Aunt Maude, who had a furnished one room bungalow located in the rear of their home. Settling in so late that evening, I decided to go straight to bed and travel to the hospital the next morning.

I will never forget feeling the combination of fear, anxiety, and stress as I entered the hospital ward—I had no idea what to expect. After receiving directions from the hospital's clerk as to where to find Daddy, I proceeded to walk slowly down the long corridor, noticing several patient beds divided by curtains. Eventually I found a nurse seated at a desk and asked for information. She politely walked with me to assist in finding my daddy. Pulling back the curtain quickly, she said, "Earl, you have a visitor."

Daddy didn't respond because he appeared to be sleeping. I immediately went over to him at the bedside and looked him in the face. To my surprise, Daddy opened his eyes and looked directly at me. "Oh, my baby," he said with a strained voice. "I'm so happy to see you."

"Daddy," I cried, "what happened?" I felt the tears well up in my eyes as I reached down to touch his hand. I thanked God that he was able to talk with me because I really didn't know what state I would find him in. However, many of my fears were alleviated for the moment as I continued to listen closely to him.

"Baby" he whispered, "I missed you!" Tears began to roll down Daddy's face.

"I'm here now, Daddy. It's okay. Don't cry." I tried to comfort him.

Daddy never smiled much, but I could tell he was relieved that I was present. He didn't look like himself. His face was dark, and he appeared to be very weak.

"Baby, I have always loved you," he said, then looked past me as if he was looking for someone. "Where is your mom?"

"She came home with me on the train, Daddy, but she wasn't able to come to the hospital." I wanted to change the subject because I knew Mom was too ashamed to come and see him. "You know Mom don't like hospitals anyway," I added.

"How you doing baby?"

"I'm doing okay, Daddy. I just got a headache right now."

Daddy looked at me, "You're still small. You never did eat right," he said. "Where's Clayton?" His voice began to change. "I don't know," I responded quickly. "When I get out of here, I am going to kill Clayton!" His facial expression became angry. "I promise you. I am going to kill him for destroying my family and my life." "Daddy, don't say that. Just pray about it. It's not worth it." Despite my attempt to change the conversation away from Clayton, Daddy was fixated on him, "I swear I'm going to do it!" he said.

I understood my daddy was overcome by hurt because of Clayton's and Mom's affair, but I so much wanted him to get over it. The emotional pain was too much for him to bear. I just wanted him to focus on getting better.

Unfortunately, it was too late for Mom and Daddy to mend their relationship because about seventy-two hours later, my precious daddy died. I truly believed he lived long enough just to say goodbye to me, and with much regret, he died brokenhearted.

As we prepared for his funeral, I continued to suffer with a headache. This was the same headache that started the day before Daddy passed away, and it never left. I took Tylenol to ease the pain, but it didn't do much good, so I managed to deal with it.

Daddy had a small life insurance policy, and I quickly turned it over to Hunt's Funeral Home. Mr. Hunt explained the process of arranging and preparing for the funeral and promised that he would put my dad away very nicely. "I'm going to give your dad a nice funeral," he said. "I'm going to treat you just like my own daughter."

Mom did not get involved with the funeral arrangements. She refused to view the body or attend the funeral because she felt too ashamed. Therefore everything was pretty much on me. Uncle Kent was supportive to me. He stood by my side during the entire funeral procession and even at the gravesite. It was a very small funeral with only a few people attending. My daddy's mother and father along with his only two sisters were already dead. His only living brother, Jack, was somewhere in Florida, but we'd lost touch and I could not find him.

Uncle Jack's family found me when I lived in Hazlehurst, through the mail system. He corresponded that the family wanted to meet me for the first time. I made arrangements to travel to Miami, Florida, where they lived. They paid for my ticket and they met me at the Greyhound bus station and took me to their home. Uncle Jack was the spitting image of my daddy; I was excited to meet him and his two daughters. I stayed with them for about a month and enjoyed the fellowship and hospitality. We went out to eat at several eateries, and they cooked for me in their home. My favorite dishes they prepared were hush puppies and catfish smothered with onions and gravy, served with rice. They also took me to Fort Lauderdale for a day's visit and we all had a great time.

I really enjoyed my visit, but after returning home to Georgia and writing a few letters to them, the mail returned to me and we lost contact. To my amazement, I never heard from them again.

After Daddy's death, Mom prepared to move back into our home on Edward Street. We slowly moved furniture into the house day by day. On the final day of moving, Mom opened the front door, and to our surprise, someone had broken in and ransacked the house! Our brand new kitchen set was gone. My personal luggage full of my clothes and other items were taken. We found out that the robbers broke through the kitchen door, which was on the back of the house.

We were so upset and hurt. Mom managed to get the doors repaired right away and changed all the locks. Although we felt violated, we knew we had to continue to live our lives as normally as possible.

Still suffering with headaches, I was beginning to feel concerned about what was actually wrong with me because they were becoming a part of my daily routine. One day I felt so bad that I could hardly hold my head up. Mom began to take notice of my complaining and started searching out different doctors to find some answers about the headaches. With much disappointment, we were unable to find any real solution or diagnosis to my problem.

Mom decided one day to take me to a Christian missionary. After explaining my story to this lady, she opened her Bible and gave me a scripture passage to quote daily. She read aloud Psalm 27:

The Lord is my light and my salvation—
whom shall I fear?
The Lord is the stronghold of my life—

of whom shall I be afraid?

When the wicked advance against me

to devour me,

it is my enemies and my foes

who will stumble and fall.

Though an army besiege me,

my heart will not fear;

though war break out against me,

even then I will be confident.

One thing I ask from the Lord,

this only do I seek:

that I may dwell in the house of the Lord

all the days of my life,

to gaze on the beauty of the Lord

and to seek Him in his temple.

For in the day of trouble

He will keep me safe in His dwelling;

He will hide me in the shelter of His sacred tent

and set me high upon a rock.

Then my head will be exalted

above the enemies who surround me;

at His sacred tent I will sacrifice with shouts of joy;

I will sing and make music to the Lord.

Hear my voice when I call, Lord;

be merciful to me and answer me.

My heart says of you, "Seek His face!"

Your face, Lord, I will seek.

Do not hide your face from me,
do not turn your servant away in anger;
you have been my helper.
Do not reject me or forsake me,
God my Savior.
Though my father and mother forsake me,
the Lord will receive me.
Teach me your way, Lord;
lead me in a straight path
because of my oppressors.
Do not turn me over to the desire of my foes,
for false witnesses rise up against me,
spouting malicious accusations.
I remain confident of this:
I will see the goodness of the Lord
in the land of the living.
Wait for the Lord;
be strong and take heart
and wait for the Lord.

After reading this psalm, the missionary anointed my head with oil and prayed for me. She encouraged Mom to continue to do the same. From that time I never went back to a doctor for headaches. Though I still experienced them from time to time, they were not as bad. Being more manageable, I learned to live with the headaches the best way I could.

CHAPTER 6

Jimmy, My Husband

AUNT MAMMY'S HUSBAND RALPH DIED AFTER A short illness. At the funeral I met Jimmy. Ralph was one of his older brothers. Now in my early twenties, I hoped for a new friend. Jimmy was in the navy and looked quite handsome and impressive wearing his dark blue uniform and white cap. He had been on leave for the funeral. Most girls back then were excited to see a man in uniform, and I was no different. The men looked so promising for a good and favorable future.

The funeral service was in Chester, but the burial was in Snowhill, Maryland. During the funeral procession to Snowhill, Jimmy and I ended up riding together in the same car. We talked the entire time, about an hour and a half drive, enjoying each other's conversation.

At the end of the day, Jimmy promised to keep in touch with me. "I am going to write you," he said as he smiled, showcasing his pearly white teeth. He watched me as I walked away, and instinctively I knew he was sincere about keeping in touch. It was not long after our initial meeting until we began to correspond with each other, marking the beginning of our lifelong relationship.

Jimmy served in the navy for a little more than three years, then received an honorable discharge after being shell-shocked. He had been stationed overseas, on the island of Okinawa, where shelling and gunfire were common. After his discharge and arriving back home, we began to date about twice a week. Jimmy and I enjoyed spending time together, especially going to the movies, which was our favorite pastime. He was a little different from my other boyfriends because he did not like attending church, but I didn't hold that against him.

One day as we walked home from the movie theater, he surprised me by the seriousness in the tone of his voice. "Baby," he said firmly, "you are going to be my wife and the mother of my children." Wow! How long have I waited for this moment. I smiled, knowing in my heart that things were serious between the two of us, and I cherished that heartfelt moment.

Jimmy and I were married in June of 1953. Our wedding was held in the living room of my family's home on Edward Street. Mom had the house fixed up really nice, but she and Ann did not attend the ceremony because they had plans to take a boat ride for the day. Still, Jimmy and I were excited about getting married because we were so much in love with each other.

Our guest list included Pastor Pyatt, who performed the ceremony, and his wife, along with my Aunt Mary. I was so grateful that my aunt attended as she was the only family member present. I needed that support. Although the wedding was short and sweet, it marked a milestone in my life. Every girl dreams of a lifelong committed relationship to a man that will love her unconditionally, to be present and supportive, and to build a family and life together. For me, I believed this person was Jimmy.

When Jimmy moved into our home, Mom let us take the front bedroom. As a new wife, I tried to make our room as attractive and comfortable as possible. Jimmy helped by purchasing a new bedroom suite and setting it up. Mom gave him the responsibility to purchase half the coal for the furnace twice a month in addition to giving her ten dollars a week in cash.

Our first daughter Cindy was born the next year, so we added a crib to the bedroom. A year later, Jimmy Jr. was born.

At first, we all got along pretty well in the house, but as the family grew, Mom and Jimmy became increasingly irritated with each other. He also started drinking more than usual, which did not help their relationship.

One night a knock came at the door. It was the police asking for Jimmy. "Can you come out for a moment, sir? Someone wants to see you," the officer said.

Jimmy looked a little nervous, not knowing exactly what was going on, but walked out to the patrol car. As he approached the car, a woman was sitting in the back seat that he appeared to be familiar with. I stood at the door, watching as she rolled down the window. He looked quite surprised. She looked out.

"The baby is sick with tonsillitis, and I want to know if you can come to the hospital with me," she asked.

Jimmy looked at the police and responded, "I'm a married man—I can't go with her." The police spoke with him for a few minutes before Jimmy came back into the house.

"Who was that?" I asked. He admitted that he had a baby with a woman named Carrie before we married, but she was not the one for him. He immediately affirmed his love and commitment to me, and I was appeased by his answer. After that evening, I never saw her again. However, I did suggest to Jimmy that he should bring the child around to get to know the family, but he was not receptive to the idea.

"I'm never going to do it," he said, and he never did. Jimmy was a stubborn man whose mind could not be changed by a woman.

A month later, we got word that Carrie had died of pneumonia. Custody of the child was turned over to the mother's sister Alice, who began to pursue Jimmy for money even more aggressively than the biological mother.

One day she came to his job to see if the money could be withdrawn from his paycheck. With no luck, she went to the court system. Jimmy became stressed about it, which led him to drown himself even more with alcohol. After work each day, he went to the state store, bought his liquor, and got with his friends to drink. By late evening, he would come home drunk as a skunk, becoming increasingly argumentative and difficult to talk to. If Jimmy did not drink, he barely communicated.

When he was stressed, he drank and became verbally abusive, and everybody around him felt it.

I tried to pacify him as much as possible when trouble came. Concerning his other child, I advised him to get money orders and mail them through the court system.

"You know it's only right to take care of your children," I said. But Jimmy did not want me involved.

"No," he responded, "all they're going to do is take my money and do what they want." Yet after much persuasion, he agreed to pay ten dollars a week through the court system for child support.

Along with the pressure of child support, Mom also asked Jimmy to help a little more around the house. She wanted him to buy all the coal each month. Jimmy did not agree with this request, which led to further tension between him and Mom.

One night we were in the bedroom discussing his contributions to the house, and Mom overheard us talking.

"With all I'm trying to do to help her, she still wants more," Jimmy yelled. "I'm not going to put up with your mother."

A knock suddenly came at the bedroom door. "Jimmy," Mom called out. She could not bear being silent any longer. "I want to talk to you Jimmy," she continued. Mom didn't sound like herself—she was angry. She pushed the door open before we could respond and entered the bedroom.

Jimmy and I were lying in bed. He quickly sat up, and both began to fire off at each other, not allowing time for either to speak or listen. They cursed each other while defending their personal opinions about the monthly bills. Finally Mom yelled, "Get out! I mean get out!" She was furious.

Everything went silent for a split second when Jimmy responded, "I'm leaving." He got up quickly, put his clothes on, and left. I felt useless in that situation and only tried to comfort the children.

We had lived with Mom for almost two years, and yes, she and Jimmy had their differences, but she never asked him to leave the home. I didn't say anything to Mom because this was her house and I respected her. Neither could I say anything to Jimmy because he was already an angry man, and with all his drinking, I didn't want him to lash out at me. I was left feeling terribly upset that evening, making it a long, sleepless night.

The next morning I wondered where he could be. Jimmy didn't have many friends, but he befriended Amos, my cousin's husband. I got dressed quickly, left the house as quietly as I could, and headed toward the east side of town, leaving the children with Mom. Arriving at my cousin's house, I knocked on the door. When the door opened, Dee looked at me as if she was expecting me to come to her home. Before I could utter a word, she said, "Jimmy's here." I immediately felt relieved.

"How are you, cousin?" I responded with a half-hearted smile.

"I'm fine. Come on in, Peas." I entered slowly, not knowing what to expect, and there he was—sitting at the dining room table talking with Amos. Jimmy was the type of man that did not like to talk about problems. He would usually end up cursing out the person who showed concerned rather than the person who offended him. So I was very careful when I began to converse with him.

"I'm sorry, baby," Jimmy said seriously while looking me in the eyes, "but I'm not coming back to your mom's house. She did not treat me fair." I listened attentively as he continued to speak, "If you want to be with me, you will have to come wherever I find a place."

"Of course I want to be with you. I love you and the kids. We should have our own place anyway," I answered. I had actually mentioned the idea of getting our own place a few times, but Jimmy never pursued the idea.

"I don't have the time to look for a place because I work every day," he said.

"I'll look," I responded.

We talked quite a bit that day, making plans for our next move together. When I finally left Dee's house, I headed across town to the Chester Newsstand to purchase the *Daily Times* paper. That same day I found an ad for an apartment at Seventh and Penn Street for rent. It was $13.50 a month with heat included.

That evening Jimmy called me at Mom's house (by this time we had telephones), and I informed him about the apartment I found in the newspaper. He complained that he did not have time to go and see it. So I agreed to check it out. The very next day I set up an appointment with Calderoni, the real estate agent, picked up the keys, and walked down to Woodrow and

Penn Street to view the apartment. After looking around, I knew I had to have Jimmy check it out because the place needed a lot of work. It was filthy! The apartment was located on the first floor, and it had three rooms. The bathroom was located on the second floor, and we would have to share it with other tenants on that level. Although it was somewhat of an eyesore, I still had a vision for the place and could see it fixed up.

When Jimmy called again, I excitedly shared what I found. "You need to come see the apartment," I said. "It's not perfect, but we can fix it up. When can you come with me to see it?"

"Where is the apartment located?" he asked.

"It's on Woodrow and Penn Street."

"Okay," he answered. "I'll come after work tomorrow to see the place."

Jimmy was anxious to see the apartment and initially went over without getting the keys. He looked through the first floor window, but unfortunately the viewing was limited, so he later asked me to obtain the keys from the agent so that we could go in together.

After work the next day, he came to Mom's house to pick me up in a cab, and we went over. I had the keys, so we were able to go right in. Once inside, Jimmy looked quite surprised, "You want this place?" he asked as he walked from room to room. "It's so dirty in here."

I quickly answered, "I can clean it up." Following him from room to room, I continued to convince him of the hidden potential of the apartment. "We can fix it up and live here for now until we find a better place."

That's exactly what happened. Later that week, Jimmy did the paperwork, secured the keys, and we were cleaning out our first home together. Jimmy-Lee, a friend of Jimmy's, came to help us clean out the old furniture and junk that was left behind. I had my bucket and mop, cleaning right behind the men. Jimmy put a fresh coat of paint on the walls, and when all was finished, everything looked amazing. It took us about two weeks to completely move out of Mom's house. This was a bittersweet time for me because I knew I would miss Mom, but I needed to be with my husband and the children with their father.

I did all the house cleaning at the apartment and even kept the bathroom clean on the second floor. The landlord came around monthly to inspect the apartment and was impressed at how we literally transformed the place.

"Y'all really fixed up this place," he said. "I never had tenants like you before. I want to do something special for you people so I'm going to build a private bathroom next to the living room."

We were so excited and surprised that he wanted to do this. We didn't expect it, but we welcomed it. He actually began the work a few weeks later. The job involved removing the living room window and replacing it with an entrance door. The bathroom was then built on the outside. It took a few weeks to complete, but it was so nice when finally finished. The landlord also decided to give us a new stove and refrigerator. He made several comments to us *over and over* again about how well we took care of his place and wished he had more tenants like us. We ended up staying at this apartment for the next five years.

As our family began to increase in size, we knew we needed a larger place. One day Jimmy came home from work full of energy, "Baby, I found a house!" He was so eager to share the news. "I found a big house on Kerlin Street." Jimmy felt we needed a big house because he wanted a lot more kids. "I need to take you over to see it. Come on!" He grabbed me by the hand, and off we went.

The house was in a nice neighborhood with only a few homes on the block. It had a nice-sized front porch and fenced-in backyard with a driveway. As we approached the house, we were greeted by an old white woman named Ms. Harper, who lived with her sister. Ms. Harper informed us that the house was set up as two apartment units—upstairs and downstairs. She lived downstairs, and her sister lived upstairs. She mentioned that the house was previously owned by a state trooper and then an obstetrician before she purchased it. This same doctor, Dr. Donahue, ended up delivering my baby daughter. When he found out about my address, he informed me that he was raised there and that the Italian owners built a wine press in the basement to make wine. This made sense because Jimmy found kegs of wine in the basement that he and his friends enjoyed when we first moved in.

On entering the main house, I noticed a small room to the

left. I immediately envisioned the children playing in this room. "Wow, this could be the playroom," I thought out loud. As we continued to walk through, we saw wooden floors throughout most of the house except for the kitchen and bathrooms, which had linoleum flooring. In addition to the front room, there was a living room, dining room, kitchen, and a full bathroom, all on the first floor. The second floor had three rooms, which also included a kitchen and full bathroom. The third floor had two bedrooms with a long hall and closet. I immediately fell in love with the house because of all the space and wanted us to buy it!

Jimmy worked at Westinghouse at the time and didn't make much money. He didn't like to broadcast to me or anyone else how much money he brought home each week. However, he gave me a lump sum every payday with instructions on what bills to pay. Although he was private about his income, he had a good habit of putting money aside and saving for a purpose.

When it came to my income, things were different. Jimmy always questioned me about the money I made and how it would be spent. I actually made four dollars per day doing days' work and had no money saved. Bottom line, we didn't have enough money to make the down payment to buy the house, but that didn't stop us from trying.

Jimmy went to speak with Ms. Harper to explain our situation. "I want the house, but I don't have enough money," he said sincerely. "We both work, we have children, and we need a secure place."

"Let's see what we can work out," she responded.

Because he was a veteran, Jimmy applied for a VA loan. Lo and behold, he was approved for $7,700, but it did not cover the complete cost of the house. We were still about $1900 short. Ms. Harper seemed anxious to sell the house and worked out a plan with Jimmy so that he could qualify for the house. She accepted the offer of the mortgage company but wrote out a separate agreement for us to pay an additional amount of $1900 to her personally. The agreement said we were buying furniture from her, which we didn't, but this was the only way she would accept the mortgage company's offer, and so we agreed to the deal.

We finally closed on buying the house, and now were considered first-time homeowners, which was a great feeling! Shortly before we moved into our new home, the city of Chester informed us that we had to remove the kitchen piping that ran to the gas stove on the second floor. This work had to be done to pass inspection because the property was purchased as a single family residence rather than an apartment.

Jimmy was so proud of our accomplishment. I could see it in his actions as he excitedly made repairs to fix up the house. We finally had something to call our own, and this was our home for the duration of our marriage.

I can truly say the first two years of our marriage were the best years. As the family grew, things changed. The first child came, then the second, next numbers three and four, and so on. I was pregnant pretty much every two years until I reached my sixth child. My children were the greatest joy in my life. However, things progressively changed between me and my husband. Jimmy was a hard-working man, but he had a serious drinking problem, which was apparent. It was his drinking that caused great stress on our marriage and family life. When he drank, he became bitter, angry, and mean. Although the marriage was deteriorating, he would always say, "I don't care what happens, this marriage will go on until death do us part."

I have always had such a great love for God, and it was my faith that helped me to deal with my home life. My relationship with Christ was my saving grace! There is no other way I could have tolerated the disappointments I found in my marriage.

One day as I walked home from work, I heard a voice in my spirit say, "If you go home, you'll never want to go there again as long as you live." I didn't understand exactly what that meant and thought it to be rather unusual. *Why am I thinking of this?* I thought to myself. Now that I look back, I believe it was the Lord warning me of what was to happen.

Anyway, I stopped at the Pantry Pride Market on Seventh Street to buy a few things, including a bottle of lemon oil furniture polish. Like Jimmy, I was excited about the new house and with our new furniture; I decided to do a little cleaning. At the time I had only four children: three girls and one son. I sat them in a circle on the floor to watch television as I began to polish the furniture. After pouring the lemon oil polish on the coffee table in the living room, I sat the bottle on the dining room table just a foot away from where I was working. As I rubbed and wiped the coffee table, I did not realize my baby girl Joy got out of the circle, went over to the dining room table, and began drinking the lemon oil polish. It must have started tasting bad or burning her throat because she screamed and threw the bottle to the floor. I ran over to her and yelled, "Oh my God, my baby is going to die!" *What can I do?* I thought. I immediately picked up Joy in my arms and ran to the kitchen sink. I tried to wash her mouth out with water, but it was not doing anything.

My son, who was about ten years old at the time, said, "Mom, you need to take her to the hospital. Call the ambulance!"

I called Jimmy, spoke with him on the phone, and explained what happened. He told me to give her some Pepto-Bismol. "She'll be all right," he said. I don't think he understood the severity of the problem, so after talking with him, I called an ambulance.

Each minute seemed like an eternity. I began to worry because the ambulance had not shown up, and I had already waited for about fifteen minutes. Joy was crying and vomiting as I held her. My son spoke up again. "Mom, call a cab!"

I was frantic and in shock, but I managed to call a cab. I left my three oldest children at home waiting for Jimmy to come in. It wasn't long before the cab arrived and he drove us to Chester Hospital at Ninth and Barclay Street, which was only a few blocks away. As we entered the emergency room, there were many patients sitting and standing around. I noticed a nurse in the corridor and tried to get her attention as I carried Joy but to no avail. She never noticed or acknowledged me. I was so nervous and didn't know what to do so I walked the halls with my baby in my arms. I became increasingly concerned because Joy was now vomiting blood. A doctor saw me and came running over to me. "Mother, what's going on?"

Before I could answer, a nurse came running out, and he began to curse at her. "Why didn't you bring this lady and her baby into the back?" The nurse tried to explain that there were many patients already in the back, waiting for care. "You never leave a mother with a crying, sick baby!" he yelled.

At that point the doctor informed me that he was going to take the baby to X-ray. He grabbed Joy out of my arms and off he went.

Meanwhile I rushed to the bathroom to wash my hands and clean the vomit off my clothes. After returning to the waiting area, I waited about fifteen more minutes before the doctor returned, this time without Joy. He advised me to follow him upstairs. As we walked together, he asked a series of questions pertaining to what happened. "What was the product?" he asked and waited for me to answer. "What were the ingredients? Where did you purchase it?" I explained everything to the best of my ability.

Joy was admitted to Chester Hospital, and they began treatment right away. The doctor informed me that the X-ray showed both lungs to be filled with poison from the lemon oil. Joy was placed on an NPO diet (nothing by mouth). The nurses started intravenous lines in her arms, with needles running into her tiny veins. She was under an oxygen tent with her eyes closed and whining faintly. It was difficult for me to eyewitness my baby in this condition at only thirteen months old because she was literally fighting for her life.

Each day, her prognosis got worse despite the many pediatric specialists that were called in on her case. Eventually they informed me that they could do no more and pretty much gave up. On about the fourteenth day at the hospital, I was sitting at Joy's bedside with my pocket-size Bible in my purse when I sensed a still, quiet voice say, "Push the Bible under the tent and let it lie on her hand." As I pushed the Bible under the tent, I closed my eyes to say a little prayer. When I opened my eyes, I noticed she opened her eyes. She looked two or three shades lighter and began to smile. She then gripped the Bible with her little hand. "You want the Bible?" I asked. I was so excited to see her responding, and I truly believed it was the Lord who spoke to me.

Joy's suffering and hospitalization became a spiritual awakening for me. I needed God to intervene! I quickly thought about Pastor Margaret Wortham at the little storefront church on Third Street called Faith Tabernacle Church. "That's where I'll go," I thought to myself. I immediately informed the nurse that I had to leave for a while but planned to return.

"Your child is very sick, and I wouldn't advise you to leave," the nurse said with a sympathetic voice yet a serious demeanor.

"But I'll be right back," I responded.

"You need to be by her side right now," she said. "Your child is too sick, and she's dying."

I trembled inside when I heard the nurse say 'dying.' I

became more determined or even desperate to seek God on behalf of my child. "I have to check on my other children," I said firmly.

"Well, who's at home with the children now?" She asked.

"My husband is home with the children, but I want to check on them too," I replied.

"Okay," she agreed, seeing I was determined. "We'll keep an eye on your baby."

I quickly left the hospital and walked as fast as I could to the church. When I arrived, I noticed a teenage boy praying at the altar. As I approached the area where he was kneeling, to my surprise he was praying for my baby! When I heard him, I fell to my knees and began to pray also. "Lord, take all of me, but save my baby. For you I live, and for you I die." I prayed and cried out desperately because I knew only God could help me. Joy needed a miracle.

When I got back home, I got a call from Mom. "Where you been?" she asked.

"I went to the store."

"Why aren't you at the hospital?"

"Mom, why haven't you gone by the hospital?" I didn't want to discuss my time at church because I felt neither she nor Jimmy would understand.

"You know how I feel about going into hospitals," she replied.

"It's okay, Mom, I have to hang up now." I was physically

drained and did not want to talk to anyone at the moment. I needed rest.

In the next few minutes I got a call from the hospital. The nurse sounded excited. "I'm calling to let you know the baby did something unusual since you left. She drank two ounces of tea by mouth. We haven't been able to get anything in her mouth since her admission fourteen days ago."

She further explained that when children drink deadly poison by mouth, it is very hard to get them to take anything further by mouth because they become fearful. I was amazed by the news and became very hopeful. My faith in God began to grow as I turned Joy over to Him.

A few days later a nurse called me around 4 a.m. "Ms. Cottman,"—I thought she mispronounced my name—"you are going to have to come and get this baby because there is nothing more we can do."

I was a little startled because Joy had been improving, and to ensure she had the right patient, I asked, "Excuse me, nurse, I'm sorry what name did you say?"

"Ms. Cottman."

I then spelled my name: "C-O-S-T-O-N."

"Oh, I'm sorry. I made a mistake. I was trying to call Ms. Cottman." At that she hung up quickly. I was a little disturbed at first that she made such a mistake, but I put it out of my mind and didn't think about it any more.

Pastor Wortham counseled me to *fast and pray* about my

situation. So for three days I ate no solid food by mouth and drank only water. This was a new experience for me.

Blessings came as I witnessed Joy's condition continue to improve each day. Finally, after twenty-five days in the hospital, she was discharged with a follow-up date set for six weeks later. The doctor admitted to me that he was amazed, "Mrs. Coston, is this the baby from the emergency room?"

"Yes, it is." I responded.

"I felt sure that you would have taken the baby home to die," he said.

"It was a miracle, doctor. God gave me a miracle."

"I don't know what you are talking about when you say miracle, but something happened and she looks good! The only precaution I have for you is that we never want to see her develop a cold for at least ten years." Upon receiving those instructions, I left the hospital with my baby, and I am happy to report Joy never experienced a common cold for ten years. To God be the glory!

This was the beginning of a changed life for me—meaning I dedicated my life to God as I shared my testimony with others about the power of prayer. I will never forget that day at church when I sought God in prayer with all of my heart for my daughter. I made a vow to Him, having every intention to keep it, and He heard my cry. As I continued to grow spiritually, my neighbors began to call on me to pray for them. Perhaps they saw something in my new life that caused them to respond that way toward me.

Although I became more active in church, at this time in my life, my activity in the church had everything to do with my personal relationship with Christ Jesus. Everything I did, I did for Him!

Pastor Wortham asked me to get the women of the church together and start a group that everyone could participate in. I came up with the idea of an outreach group to help people in the community and named it the Lending Hands. It involved a commitment to help those in need. The group lasted for only a few years but was a blessing to many. After we moved into our new church building in 1967, other programs were initiated.

Unfortunately, my marriage was still rocky at home, and my new spiritual awakening didn't help. Jimmy could not understand my new way of life and often made fun of it. I was spending more time at church, reading and studying my Bible, and developing a committed prayer life.

One day, I had just gotten home from work at about 6:30 p.m., and I began cooking dinner for my family as usual. Joy, who was much older now, came running into the house, frantic.

"Mom, come quick! The lady on the corner is sitting on the porch, and she's sick." She grabbed me by the hand. "Come on Mom," she repeated.

"Okay," I said. "Let me turn the stove off." I removed the pots from the hot burners and rushed out of the house with Joy leading the way. Immediately I noticed a woman sitting on her front porch in a rocking chair. As I approached her, she appeared pale and limp. Although I had never spoken with her, I heard she was a beautiful Christian woman and therefore felt very comfortable nearing her side. I grabbed her by the hand, and she gripped mine. I could see that she was having difficulty breathing, so I asked, "Honey, what's the matter?"

"I'm going," she said, "I'm going." Her voice was faint, but she spoke the words clearly, making a declaration about her impending death. It frightened me a little at first, and I quickly removed my hand out of her hand. Before she could say another word, she took a deep breath, slumped over in the chair and died. At that moment her son came out of the house and looked at me. "I'm going to Lee's store on the corner to get some Alka Seltzer," he said. He had no clue as to what just happened.

Alka Seltzer! I thought to myself. I looked at him in utter surprise and broke the news to him: "Honey, your mother is dead."

"I'll call an ambulance," he said, sounding shocked and a little nervous. He ran back indoors to use the phone. When the paramedics finally arrived, they checked her briefly and pronounced her dead. Being a little stunned, I left the scene to walk home and found Joy sitting on the porch.

"What happened Mom?" she asked.

"She went to the hospital," I said quietly then changed the subject, "Come on, let's get dinner ready." We both walked into the house.

My new conversion and commitment to God began to cause

many incidents like this to happen. I trusted God not only for my own situations but also for the trials and tribulations of others.

One day Ms. Della, my next door neighbor, called for me. "Come quick, come quick," she cried, "Mali collapsed on the floor and is acting as if he's losing it." She was in such a panic; I stopped what I was doing and followed her into her home. As she had described it, there was Mali on the floor, gasping for breath and vomiting. What a sight! I immediately laid my hands on him with a shout, "In the Name of Jesus!" and began to pray by the power of the Holy Spirit. A few minutes later, he was up on his feet. He was so grateful and began to thank me. I told him to give the glory to Jesus.

From that experience, Ms. Della referred me to a lady named Ms. Shallot. Apparently she had a serious problem with her neck and throat. She had already been seen by a specialist, and there were plans to do exploratory surgery at a hospital in Philadelphia. One day I went to visit her in her home, which was walking distance from my house.

Ms. Shallot was very warm and welcoming toward me and introduced me to a man whom she said was her husband. They had been together for fifteen years and were very much in love.

"I want you to pray for me," she asked. "Ms. Della told me you were a prayer warrior, and I need you to pray for me."

I was a little surprised because this was something new to me—to be referred as a "prayer warrior." I was so humbled. I got up the courage and began to pray for her and shared a few words with her that I felt were from the Lord. "Ms. Shallot," I said with confidence, "the Lord said to tell you that there will be no surgery. When you get to the hospital and they examine you, they are going to find that what was in your throat is now gone."

She became teary-eyed as I continued to speak. "Anything that you need to confess to God, confess it now so that when you go before the surgeon, you want to have everything clean."

She appeared overwhelmed with gratitude. "Thank-you, Sis, thank-you! How much do I owe you?"

I quickly answered, "Oh honey, there's never a charge to pray for the sick. We don't charge anybody for prayer." I was so surprised by her comment, I repeated, "You don't owe me anything. God is the healer; I'm just the messenger that delivered the prayer."

I didn't hear from her for the next couple of days, but when I finally talked with her, she was rejoicing.

"I went for the surgery," she said, "and they didn't have to do it because the lump was gone!" Ms. Shallot was so excited. "They couldn't find anything anywhere." At that point we began to praise the Lord together.

Ms. Shallot and her husband started attending church with me, and both decided to join. I saw Ms. Shallot becoming more serious about God and believed she was sincerely seeking a closer relationship with Him. I also noticed changes in her husband.

One day when I was visiting Ms. Shallot, her husband began

talking about his problem with drinking. He had a serious addiction to alcohol and desired to stop, but the challenge appeared too great for him to master alone. I stood in their kitchen as he talked and had the opportunity to minister to him.

"If you take the alcohol and throw the drink down the drain, you will never want another drink again," I said. He did just that! He threw his entire bottle of whiskey down the kitchen drain. Once again, God stepped in, this time to deliver Ms. Shallot's husband.

Unfortunately, they separated a few months later when Ms. Shallot confessed she wanted to do what was right.

"What do you mean?" I asked.

She said quietly, "I'm not married to him. I'm out of order, and I got to get right with God."

She eventually packed up all her belongings and left what belonged to him to start out on her own. He accepted the separation because God was dealing with him also. She went on to become a mighty prayer warrior and consecrated her life to God. She was so dedicated to prayer that she spent two years shut-in her home, fasting and praying for many people, places, and nations. I used to go to the market for her every two weeks to deliver her food. I felt good about her spiritual growth and conversion because God used me to be a part of bringing her closer to Him.

I began to witness the gospel to many men, women, boys, and girls near and far. Many made personal decisions to come to the Lord. As I watched the lives of people change, I also encountered change myself, feeling freer in my spirit. God was working on the inside of me, and it was showing on the outside, which was awesome. I found myself building healthy relationships with people, which caused many to join the church. Even if they didn't come to my church, many individuals went on to serve God on their own.

Serving at Faith Tabernacle Church was a great opportunity for many at the church. I and a few ladies, organized a food program where members had the opportunity to bring bags of food to distribute on Thanksgiving or at other special times to needy families. Because the church had a large membership at that time, we received many donations. We stored a variety of canned goods and nonperishable foods in the church's pantry cabinet. Then, a few weeks before Thanksgiving, we began to prepare baskets for community members.

It was the week of Halloween—mischief night. We were at our weekly prayer meeting on Tuesday evening when I carried two bags of food to church for the pantry cabinet. After prayer and organizing my food items, I was preparing to walk home when one of the members, a white woman driving a van, asked if I needed a ride. She went on to explain that she was taking a few members home and one had furniture on the van. "I can come back and get you," she said.

"That's all right, sister," I responded. "I'll walk home. I live just around the corner." As I prepared to leave, I noticed three hooded young men walking as I stood outside of the church gate. I looked at them, and they looked at me as they passed by but didn't say anything. I began to walk toward Parker Street, which was a block away. As I turned the corner at Third and Parker and took another few steps, I felt the Spirit speak to me: "When you get to the next corner, go up to the elderly couple's home and pretend you live there."

I thought to myself, *Lord, I'm not going to think like that; why should I think a thought like that?* I didn't realize I was being followed until I took a few more steps and looked back. I visualized two men walking and didn't make the connection that they were the hooded guys I saw a few minutes earlier. I got almost up to Fifth and Parker when another member of the church drove past and stopped with a car full of people.

"I can take you home if you want a ride," Brother Free yelled out.

"No thank-you. My house is right around the corner, but thank-you anyhow," I said and kept walking. As he drove off, I crossed the street and never looked back a second time. That's where I made a mistake! As I reached the fence where the elderly couple lived, I heard the young men begin to run in my direction, so I turned quickly and saw them catching up with me. I was a little startled and grabbed the fence with my hand when one of the guys ran past me like a whirlwind and tried to snatch my pocketbook off my shoulder, but I held on.

"Hey you guys," I yelled, "you better stop and mind your own business." I ran up on the porch, almost physically shaking when I began to knock and bang on the glass storm door. I watched the guys run out of sight when they turned the corner at the end of the block. I was scared when no one answered the door, nor was anyone in sight even though it was about nine thirty at night. I looked at a field behind the couple's house and thought, *Oh my God, I can't run there!* Running to the field would not be safe. They could kill me and leave me on the railroad track located back in that area. I needed to get home as fast as I could.

I began to run toward my house, which was about a block away, and as I approached my neighbor's house, I noticed a pile of bricks on the steps. When I looked up, I saw the same guys trying to break into my neighbor's house through a window. My neighbor must have heard them because the kitchen light came on and the guys began to run again.

They saw me, as I was just one door away from my house, and ran directly toward me to encircle me. If they pick up those bricks, I could get hurt, I thought. I was extremely frightened and so I screamed loudly: "the blood of Jesus!" I believed I startled them for a moment by the loud outburst because somehow I managed to get out of the circle.

Next I attempted to run into the street, but I fell and hit my knee on the curb. I tried to get up, but one of the men pushed me back down onto the pavement, and I felt the most excruciating pain in my left knee and couldn't get up. This was the worst pain I have experienced in my life! One of the men bent down on his hands and knees to grab my pocketbook off my shoulder. "Oh my God!" I whispered and looked directly in his eyes because I had about a thousand dollars in cash in my purse—I had just gotten paid from work that day.

The other two men stood looking down on me, and one of them spoke up. "Come on, man, let's get out of here." I was amazed when the man released my bag as the strap reached my wrist. He made no further attempt to take it off, and finally all three men ran off. The Lord showed me that day that there is power in the Blood of Jesus.

I laid on the ground in front of my house in shock. After a few minutes, I managed to yell out, "Janet!" My daughter's room was on the third floor, so I yelled a little louder. "Janet!" She looked out the window, and my family came running. Joy was first to come out of the house, screaming and crying.

"Mommy, Mommy, are you alright?" she cried frantically.

"I'm okay. I just need some help," I said as calmly as I could, trying to appease my daughter's distress.

They called an ambulance, and by the time it arrived, as they were preparing to take me to the hospital, Jimmy drove up. He was drunk as a skunk. He pulled halfway up into the driveway and jumped out of the car, yelling and cursing at me while I attempted to explain what was happening.

He turned to the paramedics, "Take her to Sacred Heart Hospital, not Crozer." Jimmy was incoherent, and they didn't know what to think.

I pleaded with the paramedics, "Please just take me to the hospital. Don't pay any attention to him." They took me to Crozer.

I wasn't there but a short time when Pastor Wortham came in to see me. Apparently my older children called to notify her because I know it wasn't Jimmy. She immediately rushed to my bedside, took out a bottle of blessed oil, threw the oil on me, and began to pray. She had already conversed with the doctors, who informed her that they planned on taking me to surgery in the morning.

"Jimmy is out in the waiting room carrying on," she whispered.

"Pay him no mind," I responded and immediately changed the subject. "Pastor, I never wanted to have surgery," I murmured.

The pastor listened attentively. "Let's pray about it," she said. She was such a comfort and support to me.

A doctor finally came in and laid out the plan to me regarding surgery. It was just as the pastor had spoken, so I felt there was nothing I could do but wait for that time to come.

Around seven thirty the next morning, a whole team of doctors gathered around my bed. One said: "Mrs. Coston, we have changed our diagnosis for you. We are not going to do the surgery. We decided to draw out fluid from your knee and then put you in a cast and see how that works. In time you will probably get arthritis, but for now: no surgery!"

God heard my cry! I remained in the hospital for seven days. Then I was discharged to home and was confined to a hospital bed that was set up in my living room.

Pastor Wortham informed me about the Victims Crime Commission, an organization that helped people financially who had been victimized. I checked it out right away. After a few weeks, I was able to get an application, which required my doctor and employer to fill out some forms in order for me to qualify. I returned the application and had to wait.

Jimmy was excited to find out that I qualified for funding and began to watch the mail every day. "I'm going to take that check," he said.

I never said a word because his alcoholic condition was at its' worse, including his attitude toward me. Jimmy described himself as caring for me while I laid in bed with a full leg cast. I certainly needed a little help each day but his mood swings and offensive tone of voice escalated as he drank. He became verbally abusive by the end of each day because of his drunkenness. At first I couldn't figure out how he was getting drunk since he stayed with me the entire day. But pretty soon I realized he was sneaking drinks throughout the day and hiding his bottle of liquor under his chair or in different parts of the house.

Jimmy had stopped working a few months before my incident because he was not physically able to keep up the pace at work due to his drinking. He was quickly running out of money, and this check from the commission meant a lot to him. He became increasingly angry when the check did not come fast enough. He was also suspicious of me and would not leave my bedside for a minute. That I couldn't figure out.

Each day I watched the *700 Club* on television, which was inspiring and encouraging to me. I often called them for prayer, and on one particular day I received a call from their office. A woman representative called to have prayer with me. As she began to pray and speak the word of the Lord to me, Jimmy jumped up from the couch and came over to the bed. When I first noticed him coming over, I interrupted her, not knowing what he was going to do. "Thank-you," I blurted out, and before I could hang up, the phone went dead because he snatched it out of my hand.

"I know what you were doing all that time," he said with a frown. "You were talking with that holy, sanctified ..." He then began to imitate me speaking in tongues. I just listened as he ranted and raged about nonsense.

Such behavior was ongoing and happened every day! Lying in bed, unable to do much on my own and deal with his shenanigans, was insanity to me, a bit too much for me to take. Secretly, I talked to the Lord about it. People just don't know what I went through.

One day my son and I returned home from physical therapy. Little Jim was a great help to me. I called upstairs to let Jimmy know that I was home, but there was no answer. I called and called. "Jimmy, Jimmy, I'm home."

His car was in the driveway, so he had to be home. I took my time and climbed the steps as carefully as I could with my leg cast still in place. When I finally reached the second floor and passed the bathroom, I noticed blood on the floor near the toilet. I stepped into to the bedroom, and there was Jimmy, lying across the bed naked. I immediately noticed the wall near his side of the bed splattered with what appeared to be bloody vomit. I called out to him, "Jimmy, Jimmy what happened?"

"I don't know," he murmured.

"I'm calling the paramedics."

"No, don't call. I'll be all right."

"No, I'm calling," I insisted. I picked up the house phone and dialed the paramedics. In about ten minutes, two white paramedics came up to the bedroom and told Jimmy that they would be taking him to the hospital.

"Mr. Jimmy, we are here to help you," one of the paramedics said.

"No! I'm not going nowhere," he stubbornly announced.

"Please, Jimmy, go with them to get checked out," I pleaded.

"No! I'll be all right." Jimmy said.

The paramedics said to me that there was nothing they could do. He had a right to refuse to go to the hospital. After I pleaded with them and informed them of his alcohol addiction, they decided to try to get someone else to talk with him.

A few minutes later, a local black cop came in, someone Jimmy recognized.

"Come on, baby, you have to get to the hospital," the cop said with confidence and authority. "Come on, let's get your clothes on."

Jimmy responded positively to him and began to move. The paramedics were then able to take him in the ambulance with the help of the police officer.

This event happened around Valentine's Day in 1980. Jimmy

laid in Crozer Hospital on his death bed. I was still on crutches at the time but I faithfully stood by his side. The only thing I can remember saying to him when he took a turn for the worse was to lead him in the sinner's prayer. As I attentively watched his face, I noticed a tear coming down his cheek. I then squeezed his hand and he gripped mine. I truly believe he finally surrendered to Christ on that day. Jimmy stayed in the hospital for about seven days before he passed.

Jimmy was the man who worked to keep a roof over our heads, food on the table, and clothes on our backs. This is the man I dedicated myself to in marriage and stood by his side to take care of our children and our home. Despite our trials and tribulations in marriage, we stayed together and kept our vows because Jimmy made up in his mind: "until death do us part." This is the man who I loved and who loved me to the best of his ability.

It was not long after Jimmy's death when I received a check from the Victims Crime Commission for about three thousand dollars. This was a lot of money in those days. It was still hard for me to believe that after twenty-seven years of marriage, Jimmy had gone into eternity.

Whenever someone talks to me about remarrying, my response is always *"No way!"* I will marry only once in my lifetime and I plan to keep that commitment. I never desired a second marriage because in the first place, I didn't want anybody else over my kids. Also, I knew of a few people who had bad experiences. Besides, the Lord was telling me that a second marriage would be no good for me.

With so many bad memories in our home, I began to make plans to move immediately following Jimmy's death. It didn't take long to find a three-bedroom house on the other side of town. And so, in July of that year, the kids and I packed up to move, and we never looked back.

After Jimmy's death, my life changed. Although I mourned the death of my husband, I felt so free! I rededicated my total life to God and served Him like never before. This truly was a turning point in my life, and I began to grow and blossom in ministry.

I thank God for the opportunities to serve in the church where He planted me – Faith Tabernacle Church. It has been such a blessing to my life.

Pastor Wortham assigned me to be the Pastor's Aid President, and a year later, the Missionary President.

As Pastor's Aid President, I encouraged members to support and serve our pastor. We truly strived to hold up the arms of our leaders and ensure that our pastors had whatever they needed to do the will of God. I served in this position for more than thirty-five years.

As Missionary President, I led the charge in sending monthly support to our local and foreign missionaries, men and women of God who served faithfully in spreading the gospel. I will never forget our support for Ralph and Justine Lampkins, who were missionaries in Liberia, Africa, and Elder Jetters along with his family in Nova Scotia, Canada. These two families were dedicated to missions, and we faithfully supported their work. Having a true love for missions made it easy for me to serve in this post for so many years.

I was also involved in a city-wide effort to support pastors. I started a Pastors Aid Board, but it lasted only a year. Group members from a variety of churches desired to raise money and be a blessing to their pastors, but something happened such that it was stopped. I never really understood what took place that stopped this ministry.

Serving as a member of Women's Aglow International for two years was such a privilege. Dorothy Harris spearheaded this chapter in the city of Chester as we met monthly to have Bible study and discussions. This group was also committed to assisting community members who had special needs.

I attended many events for the Prayer Band of Chester. Although I was not an official member, I always had a passion for prayer and enjoyed the services. With the many responsibilities to my own church, I began to have little time for outside activities with other churches or organizations.

Housekeeping and cooking are my personal career choices in life. I love cleaning and cooking because it comes so natural for me! I also perform these duties on a regular basis at my church along with decorating for special events or holidays, which helps to beautify the sanctuary.

Today, I still reside in Chester; I am so passionate about God and sold out completely to His will and purpose for my life. I live for Him only! When I quote my favorite scripture passage, Psalm 27, it continually refreshes my spirit and soul thereby worthy of repeating. It states:

The Lord is my light and my salvation—
whom shall I fear?
The Lord is the stronghold of my life—
of whom shall I be afraid?
When the wicked advance against me
to devour me,
it is my enemies and my foes
who will stumble and fall.
Though an army besiege me,
my heart will not fear;
though war break out against me,
even then I will be confident.
One thing I ask from the Lord,
this only do I seek:
that I may dwell in the house of the Lord
all the days of my life,
to gaze on the beauty of the Lord
and to seek Him in his temple.
For in the day of trouble
He will keep me safe in His dwelling;
He will hide me in the shelter of His sacred tent
and set me high upon a rock.
Then my head will be exalted

above the enemies who surround me;
at His sacred tent I will sacrifice with shouts of joy;
I will sing and make music to the Lord.
Hear my voice when I call, Lord;
be merciful to me and answer me.
My heart says of you, "Seek His face!"
Your face, Lord, I will seek.
Do not hide your face from me,
do not turn your servant away in anger;
you have been my helper.
Do not reject me or forsake me,
God my Savior.
Though my father and mother forsake me,
the Lord will receive me.
Teach me your way, Lord;
lead me in a straight path
because of my oppressors.
Do not turn me over to the desire of my foes,
for false witnesses rise up against me,
spouting malicious accusations.
I remain confident of this:
I will see the goodness of the Lord
in the land of the living.
Wait for the Lord;
be strong and take heart
and wait for the Lord.

At eighty-eight years young today, there are a few things that I sincerely enjoy. I enjoy getting up in the morning and driving to work because I truly love my jobs. I enjoy when my birthday comes around every Fourth of July because it's a time of celebration for me and my family, and I truly love my family. I enjoy telling people that my favorite color includes all shades of blue and that my favorite song which I love is "Have Thine Own Way." I also enjoy visiting my favorite vacation spot, which is located in my birth state of Georgia: a city called Atlanta. I truly love Atlanta, Georgia.

I've had some good days and I've had some bad days but I still have joy! And the secret to the joy I experience each day lies in my personal relationship with Jesus Christ. As a seasoned saint my desire is to be obedient to the Spirit of Christ. I always pray first and am led by the Holy Spirit in whatever I do. As a mother in the church and an elder in my community, I have the opportunity to speak *life* into the lives of many people every day and I advise them all, "Stay focused on Jesus; He is the only way!"

As I sum up everything that is written in this book concerning me and my family, I look back and realize that God has held me in His Hand from the very beginning. Although this Christian journey has not always been a smooth ride, because of Christ, I have experienced victory as I continue to pray, stand, and embrace His Living Word. It has been a great source of comfort and guidance for me and I know the same can happen for you. So in closing, I leave you with this scripture:

Therefore, my dear brothers and sisters, stand firm. Let nothing move you. Always give yourselves fully to the work of the Lord, because you know that your labor in the Lord is not in vain. (1 Corinthians 15:58 NIV)

Blessings to all who read this book!

Printed in the United States
By Bookmasters